EY

KU-638-371

EL

TOP 10
PROVENCE
& THE CÔTE D'AZUR

ROBIN GAULDIE
ANTHONY PEREGRINE

DK Penguin Random House

Top 10 Provence and the Côte d'Azur Highlights

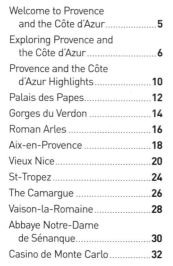

The Top 10 of Everything

CONTENTS

Provence and the Côte d'Azur Area by Area

Streetsmart

Within each Top 10 list in this book, no hierarchy of quality or popularity is implied. All ten are, in the editor's opinion, of roughly equal merit.

Front cover and spine *Lovely view of Saignon with lavender fields in bloom, Provence*
Back cover *Calanques d'En Vau, a picturesque inlet near Cassis, Provence*
Title page *The Calanque de Sormiou, near Marseille*

Welcome to
Provence and the Côte d'Azur

Provence is the most dazzling corner of France. The region's perfect light drew artists such as Renoir and Matisse, while its Riviera glamour has enchanted famous names from Grace Kelly to Kate Moss. It is a place of history and mystery, fantastic food and unbridled fun. With Eyewitness Top 10 Provence & the Côte d'Azur, it's yours to explore.

Thousands of years of migration have left a lasting cultural legacy in Provence, and historic sites such as the Roman amphitheatre in **Nîmes**, the medieval **Abbaye de Sénanque** and the papal vineyards of **Châteauneuf-du-Pape** still operate today. The 20th century shone an even stronger spotlight on the region's timeless villages and towns. Picasso painted Antibes, Van Gogh lost an ear in Arles, and Cézanne captured the Provencal countryside around Aix-en-Provence on canvas.

The Côte d'Azur is the south of France at its most cosmopolitan and lively, from the gaming tables of **Monaco** to the topless beaches of **St-Tropez**. If you grow tired of the high life, it is easy to escape to the perched villages of the **Alpes-Maritimes** and the **Var**, to the wild **Camargue** wetlands or to the **Îles de Lérins** off Cannes. The region is filled with places where you can savour your own off-the-beaten-track paradise.

Whether you're visiting for a weekend or a week, our Top 10 guide brings together the best of everything the region has to offer, from the museums of **Marseille** to the nightlife in **Nice**. The guide gives you tips throughout, from seeking out what's free to avoiding the crowds, as well as ten easy-to-follow itineraries designed to cover a clutch of sights in a short space of time. Add inspiring photography and detailed maps, and you've got the essential pocket-sized travel companion. **Enjoy the book, and enjoy Provence and the Côte d'Azur.**

Clockwise from top: **The fishing port of Cassis; carved stonework at Église St-Trophime, Arles;** flamingoes in the Carmargue; the Calanque d'En-Vau, Cassis; interior of Notre-Dame de la Garde, Marseille; Les Arénes, Arles; cypress trees at Château de Berne

Exploring Provence and the Côte d'Azur

Provence's most important sights are scattered widely across the region, but a world-class public transport system, with the Nice-Cannes-Aix-Marseille-Avignon TGV train along its spine, connects every hilltop village and coastal town. Here are some ideas to help you make the most of your time.

Two Days in Provence

Day ❶

MORNING

Start your day in **Nice** (see pp94–9) with a stroll down **cours Saleya** (see p20). Marvel at the Marche aux Fleurs (flower market), the city's most colourful sight (Tue–Sun), then take a jaunt down the **promenade du Paillon** (see pp94–5).

AFTERNOON

After a lunch of *salade Niçoise* on the seafront promenade des Anglais, relive the French Riviera's glamorous past in the **Villa Masséna** (see p96).

Day ❷

MORNING

Take an early TGV train to explore Avignon's historic **Palais de Papes** (see pp12–13), which overlooks the River Rhône. Have lunch at the venerable **Hiely-Lucullus** (see p131).

AFTERNOON

Hire a car and drive through lavender fields to the Roman town of **Vaison-la-Romaine** (see pp28–9). Complete the day with a walk around the bucolic **Abbaye Notre-Dame de Sénanque** (see pp30–31).

Seven Days in Provence

Day ❶

As Day 1 of Two Days in Provence.

Day ❷

Nothing says **Nice** (see pp94–9) like Henri Matisse. Take coffee below his former apartment (at what is now Bar L'F, pl Charles Félix), and head up Cimiez hill to marvel at the countless works he bequeathed to the city, now in the **Musée Matisse** (see p44).

Nice's promenade du Paillon offers a leafy stroll in the heart of the busy city.

Vaison-la-Romaine

GARD

VAUCLUSE

Abbaye Notre-Dame de Sénanque

Avignon, Palais de Papes

TGV

St Remy-de-Provence

BUS

Les Baux-en-Provence

Arles

BOUCHES-DU-RHONE

TGV

Camargue

Aix-en-Provence

TGV

0 km   20

0 miles   20

St-Tropez harbour is lined with fishing boats and super-yachts.

Key
- Two-day itinerary
- Seven-day itinerary

After lunch, ride the coastal train 15 minutes east to spin the wheel of fortune at the fabled **Casino de Monte Carlo** (see pp32–3).

Day ❸
Take a boat west along the coast for a lazy day on the sands of **St-Tropez's** La Fontanette beach. Later, try your hand at *pétanque* on places des Lices, then celebrity-spot around the Vieux Port (see pp24–5).

Day ❹
Head north to **Aix-en-Provence** (see 18–19) and follow in the footsteps of Paul Cézanne to the artist's favourite restaurant, the Brasserie Les Deux Garçons on cours Mirabeau. Pick up a Passeport Cézanne to lead you to some other key sights, including the Atelier Cézanne (his studio, just as he left it) and his family home, the Bastide du Jas de Bouffan.

Day ❺
Start out early. It's a long – if visually stunning – drive northeast to visit the **Gorges du Verdon** (see pp14–15 & 121). Stop en route for a bite to eat, and then tour the Corniche Sublime by car. This hair-raising road loops past the Balcons de la Mescla viewpoint, some 700 m (2,300 ft) above the canyon floor. Make sure you save enough time for a hired boat trip out onto **Lac de Ste-Croix** (see p91) before you return to Aix for the night.

Day ❻
Take an early train through the vineyards from Aix to **Arles** (see pp16–17). Play gladiator in the Roman amphitheatre then picnic amid the ruins. Arles is also the gateway to the breathtaking **Camargue** (see pp26–7). Cycle, kayak or take a boat tour to see flamingoes and other birdlife, white horses and black bulls.

Day ❼
Take a bus to **St-Rémy-de-Provence** (see p83) with its street markets and pavement cafés, which were so loved by local resident Vincent van Gogh. Copies of his paintings are displayed where they were painted, along a picturesque artist's trail. A short bus ride further, **Les Baux-de-Provence** (see p82) boasts a dramatic ruined castle, several Michelin-starred restaurants and panoramic views over the Provence countryside.

Top 10 Provence and the Côte d'Azur Highlights

Abbaye Notre-Dame de Sénanque, surrounded by lavender fields

🔟 Provence and the Côte d'Azur Highlights

Provence's top sights span the region's rich and varied history, from Roman arenas and isolated abbeys to the opulence of the *belle époque* and the chic resorts beloved of the 20th-century jet set. Sun-soaked beaches, pretty villages and a mountainous interior have drawn generations of artists, and continue to enchant visitors today.

Palais des Papes ①
This medieval palace, the seat of 14th-century pontiffs, dominates the delightful town of Avignon *(see pp12–13)*.

② Gorges du Verdon
The Verdon river flows through deep limestone gorges into the Lac de Ste-Croix, creating one of Provence's most stunning natural landscapes *(see pp14–15)*.

③ Roman Arles
Arles was one of the Roman Empire's most important cities, and its splendid arena still evokes the age of Caesar *(see pp16–17)*.

Aix-en-Provence ④
Aix is packed with museums and historic buildings. Nearby Mont Sainte-Victoire inspired the Provençal artist Cézanne *(see pp18–19)*.

5 Vieux Nice
Nice is a lively and sophisticated city, but its Old Quarter retains a more authentic character (see pp20–21).

6 St-Tropez
Pretty and chic St-Tropez, with its yacht-filled harbour and fantastic beaches, is the place to see and be seen on the Provençal coast (see pp24–5).

7 The Camargue
Vast lagoons inhabited by flamingoes and plains with black bulls are just part of the protected landscape of the regional natural park of the Camargue (see pp26–7).

8 Vaison-la-Romaine
A treasury of archaeological finds has been unearthed in this small town, once one of Provence's most important Roman towns (see pp28–9).

9 Abbaye Notre-Dame de Sénanque
The great Cistercian abbey is a fine example of Romanesque religious architecture (see pp30–31).

10 Casino de Monte Carlo
Walk in the footsteps of princes and film stars at the Riviera's most dazzling example of 19th-century grandeur (see pp32–3).

TOP 10 ⭐ Palais des Papes

In 1309, Pope Clement V transferred the papacy to France to escape political turmoil in Rome, and, for 68 years, Avignon became the religious and political centre of Christendom. The magnificent Papal Palace was built in just over 20 years, begun in 1335. Pope Benedict XII was responsible for the sober, Cistercian architecture of the Old Palace; his successor, Clement VI, added the New Palace in Gothic style, creating a massive ensemble of towers and stone walls soaring 50 m (165 ft) above the town centre. It remains a monument to the vast power of the papacy in the Middle Ages.

3 Consistory Hall

It was in the vast Salle du Consistoire that the pope, cardinals and dignitaries gathered to consider key issues of the day. It is now a museum of artifacts from around the palace **(left)**, including elegant 14th-century frescoes by Simone Martini.

Palais des Papes

1 Courtyard of Honour

The "meeting" of the two palaces is the best place to compare their respective styles. While the Old Palace resembles a defensive keep, the New Palace has finer stonework. Today the courtyard is the venue for theatrical events taking place during the Avignon Festival (see p70).

2 St John's Chapel

Just off the Consistory Hall, this decorative gem was created by Matteo Giovanetti, a leading Sienese artist. The now faded frescoes depict the lives of St John the Baptist and St John the Evangelist with exceptional use of perspective across the walls and arched vault.

4 Refectory

It was in the large refectory (tinel) that the pope entertained on feast days, such as a cardinal's appointment or a papal coronation. The pope would eat alone on a dais, while cardinals and guests were arranged around the room according to rank. The spectacular barrel-vaulted wooden ceiling was restored in the 1970s.

5 Stag Room

Clement VI let his extravagant tastes run wild in his study **(below)**. Frescoes of hunting and fishing in a forest setting cover the walls – the most unusual decor in the palace.

⑥ Benedict XII's Cloister

These four connecting buildings, surrounding a courtyard, date from 1340. Used for staff and guest accommodation, they were decorated by the Italian artist Simone Martini. The Benedictine chapel is also here.

⑨ Great Chapel

Of massive proportions, 52 m (170 ft) long, 15 m (50 ft) wide and 20 m (65 ft) high, with seven vaulted bays, the Grande Chapelle was the scene of all kinds of religious celebrations, including papal coronations.

⑦ Treasury Halls

The papal wealth was stashed beneath the flagstoned floor of the Lower Treasury Hall. The Upper Treasury Hall was effectively the accounts department.

⑩ Pope's Chamber

The pope's bedroom gives a sense of everyday palace life. The pontiffs slept within blue walls decorated with vine and oak-leaf motifs **(below)**.

⑧ Great Audience Hall

This was the meeting place of the popes' forbidding judiciary, against which no appeal was allowed. The vaulted ceiling bears a small section of the Fresco of the Prophet – sadly, much of it was hacked off and sold while the palace was a barracks in the 19th century.

PAPAL AVIGNON

The arrival of the papacy in Avignon brought great wealth and prestige to the town. When Pope Gregory XI took the papacy back to Rome in 1377 the French cardinals did not approve. On his death, they elected a French pope, while Italian cardinals elected an Italian one, putting the Christian world in schism. The row was resolved in 1417 and Avignon popes after Gregory XI have been considered anti-popes.

NEED TO KNOW

MAP B3
- Pl du Palais, Avignon
- 04 32 74 32 74,
- www.palais-des-papes.com

Open daily; Nov–Feb: 9am–5:45pm; Mar: 9am–6:30pm; Apr–Jun: 9am–7pm, Jul: 9am–8pm, Aug: 9am–8:30pm, Sep–Oct: 9am–7pm.

Adm €11; under-8s free

- Arrive early in the morning to avoid the crowds – the palace receives up to 4,000 visitors a day in summer.

- There is a great café on the roof of the palace, serving a range of drinks and snacks.

- The palace's excellent hand-held audio-guides are available in 11 languages (€2).

- Ask for the Avignon Passion when buying your first ticket to any Avignon sight – it entitles you to discounts of 10–50 per cent on entrance to other sites.

TOP 10 ★ Gorges du Verdon

The aptly named Gorges du Verdon is one of the most spectacular sights in France. Cutting deep into the rock, the Verdon river has created a series of canyons 25 km (15 miles) long and up to 700 m (2,300 ft) deep – a geography that prevented the area being fully explored until 1905. Vividly blue in places, foaming white where it storms through rapids beneath limestone cliffs, the Verdon flows south into the turquoise waters of the Lac de Ste-Croix, formed by damming the river close to Ste-Croix village. For the daring, the canyon offers rock climbing, whitewater rafting and hiking, while the 140-km (85-mile) drive around its magnificent landscapes takes a full day.

2 Point Sublime

Close to the village of Rougon, Point Sublime is one of the best places to look down into the rugged landscapes of the gorge. From here, the GR4 trail leads down into the canyon. Sturdy footwear is required, as is a torch (flashlight) to explore the tunnels cut into the cliffs.

3 La Corniche Sublime

The drive along the Corniche Sublime (D71), on the south side of the canyon, genuinely lives up to its name. Stop at the Balcons de la Mescale for a superb view and marvel at Europe's highest bridge, the Pont de l'Artuby, at 125 m (410 ft) high.

4 Moustiers-Sainte-Marie

This lovely village appears to grow out of the surrounding cliffs, with graceful stone bridges connecting houses on either side of the Ravine de Notre-Dame. Noted for its earthenware, it has a small museum and a 12th-century cliffside church, the Chapelle de Notre-Dame-de-Beauvoir (see pp48 &119).

1 Route des Crêtes

The Route des Crêtes requires a good head for heights and close attention to the road, but rewards visitors with unbeatable vertiginous views across the most spectacular reaches of the canyon (above).

Gorges du Verdon

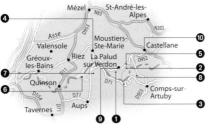

5 Martel Trail

Forming part of the much longer GR4 walking trail through the canyon, the Martel Trail (above) is the most popular hike through the gorges, passing dizzying cliffs and crossing narrow passes (see p65).

8 Trigance
This small, attractive village, with its fine views of the rugged mountain peaks that surround it, is a good place to stop for lunch on a motoring tour of the canyon.

9 La Palud sur Verdon
La Palud (see p122) is the base for organized walking expeditions into the canyon, whitewater rafting and kayaking on the rapids.

10 Castellane
The pleasant, small town of Castellane is the largest community in the area and has the widest choice of places to stay and eat. Tour operators here offer a range of activities in the canyon (see p122).

6 Lac de Ste-Croix
The hydroelectric dam that created this 10-km (6-mile) long lake **(above)**, south of Moustiers, generates much of Provence's power supply. Electric motorboats, canoes, windsurf boards and catamarans can be hired at Ste-Croix, Les Salles and Bauduen.

7 Aiguines
A stately 17th-century château, with tiled roofs and white turrets **(below)**, overlooks this attractive village. There are panoramic views over the lake.

NEED TO KNOW

Office du Tourisme:
MAP E3 ■ Pl de l'Eglise, Moustiers-Ste-Marie
■ 04 92 74 67 84
■ www.moustiers.eu

Open daily; Apr–Jun, Sep: 10am–noon, 2–6pm; Jul–Aug: 9:30am–7pm (9:30am–12:30pm, 2– 7:30pm Sat & Sun); Mar, Oct–Nov: 10am–noon, 1:30–5:30pm;

Dec–Feb: 10am–noon, 1:30–5pm

Office du Tourisme:
MAP F3 ■ Rue Nationale, Castellane ■ 04 92 83 61 14
■ www.castellane-verdontourisme.com

Open Sep–Jun: 9am–noon, 2–6pm Mon–Sat (May–Jun, Sep: 10am–1pm Sun); Jul–Aug: 9am–7:30pm daily

■ Hôtel du Grand Canyon (Corniche Sublime/D71, Aiguines, 04 94 76 91 31) is a good lunch spot with a breathtaking view. Specialities include *poulet aux écrevisses* (chicken with freshwater crayfish).

■ During Apr–Sep, white-water rapid raft trips can be taken down the canyon. Book with an operator in Castellane.

TOP 10 ★ Roman Arles

One of the region's most charming towns, Arles was founded by Greek traders but soon gained favour with Caesar and his successors. Its location, on the ancient Via Domitia at the southernmost crossing point of the dangerous river Rhône, saw it grow into one of the most important provincial cities of the Roman Empire. Like many towns of the era, it was built to resemble a miniature version of Rome, with all the amenities. Some of these survive, impressively intact, in the city centre, including the remnants of a Roman theatre, baths and an arena where gladiatorial contests were staged.

Les Arènes ①

One of the most spectacular Roman relics in Provence, this well-preserved arena **(right)** has two floors of arches and seats for 12,000 spectators.

② Porte de la Redoute and Tour des Mourgues

These battered gate towers stand either side of the former Via Aurelia, the highway which ran all the way from Arles to Rome.

③ Église St-Trophime

This spectacular Romanesque church **(left)**, with its beautiful carved stonework, was originally devoted to St Stephen. In the 10th century it became the church of St Trophimus *(see p46)*.

④ Thermes de Constantin

A semi-circular apse marks the site of the once palatial bathhouse built in the 4th century, in the reign of Emperor Constantine.

⑤ Cryptoporticus du Forum

This amazing labyrinth of chambers beneath the ancient Forum was the city's granary, carved out of the ground during the 1st century AD.

Théâtre Antique ⑥

All that now remains of the Roman theatre, once the hub of Arles, are these two graceful columns **(right)**, also known as the "two widows".

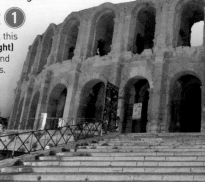

ARLES BULLFIGHTS

Les Arènes was built to stage the gory gladiator contests so loved by the Romans, and today is still the scene of battles between man and beast. During the bullfighting season, every seat in the arena is filled. Most contests are Provençal-style, in which the bull is not harmed, although Spanish-style *corridas* do also take place.

7 Musée Départemental Arles Antique

Highlights of the finest collection of Roman sculpture in Provence include a statue of Venus and a massive Altar of Apollo. There's also a Roman barge that was found on the bed of the Rhône river.

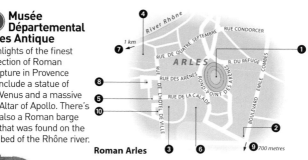

Roman Arles

9 Les Alyscamps

This long avenue of marble sarcophagi marks the site of the Roman necropolis where the city's dignitaries were buried. Among the many legends surrounding the site, it is claimed that Christ appeared here at the burial of St Trophimus, the first bishop of Arles.

8 Place du Forum

Nothing remains today but the name of the Forum, the market which was the very heart of Roman Arles. However the Place du Forum is still the hub of the town.

10 Egyptian Obelisk

Decorated with sculpted lions **(right)**, the square-sided obelisk is likely to have been a trophy from Rome's conquest of Egypt during the reign of Augustus.

NEED TO KNOW

MAP B4

Les Arènes: rondpoint des Arènes. **Open** daily; Apr & Oct: 9am–6pm; May, Jun–Sep: 9am–7pm; Nov–Mar: 10am–5pm. Closed 1 Jan, 1 May, 1 Nov, 25 Dec. Adm €8

Musée Départemental Arles Antique: av 1ère Division France Libre. **Open** 10am–6pm

Wed–Mon. Closed 1 Jan, 1 May, 1 Nov, 25 Dec. Adm €8

Thermes de Constantin: rue du Grand Prieuré. **Open** daily; Apr & Oct: 9am–6pm, May–Sep: 9am–7pm; Nov–Mar: 10am–5pm. Closed 1 Jan, 1 May, 1 Nov, 25 Dec. Adm €3

Les Alyscamps: av des Alyscamps. **Open** daily; times are

the same as for Thermes de Constantin. Adm €3.50

Cryptoporticus du Forum: pl de la Republique. **Open** daily; times are the same as for Thermes de Constantin. Adm €3.50

■ You can save on entry fees with a Pass Liberté, available from the tourist office for €11. It allows entry to up to five sights and is valid for one month.

TOP 10 ★ Aix-en-Provence

Aix-en-Provence is a sophisticated town. Whether in the dignified squares and little streets of the Old Quarter or amid the elegant town houses and tree-lined avenues of the 17th- and 18th-century district, the atmosphere is self-consciously graceful. But it's also lively and fresh: students, studying at one of France's oldest universities, are ubiquitous. The calendar of artistic events is rich, and the markets are the best in the region. The Romans called the town "Aquae Sextius", after the thermal springs which still flow here.

Cours Mirabeau ①
Created in 1650, Aix's majestic main avenue **(right)** is a tunnel of greenery created by giant plane trees. In their shade stand tall town houses and, on the northern side, smart, lively cafés. A series of fountains adds freshness to the grandeur.

② Rue Gaston-de-Saporta
Running from the town hall to the cathedral is the liveliest thoroughfare of the Old Quarter, buzzing with commerce.

③ Atelier Cézanne
Cézanne's studio, from 1902 until his death, has been left as it was – a jumble of artist's tools, furniture and still-life subjects **(above)**.

④ Mont Sainte-Victoire
This mountain **(below)** east of Aix, at 1,000 m (3,300 ft) high and 7 km (11 miles) across, exerts an almost mystical power over the region. Cézanne was so obsessed by its changing moods that he painted it more than 60 times. On its northern slopes is the Château de Vauvenargues, former home and burial place of Picasso *(see p41)*.

EXPLORING AIX

Start at the Office du Tourisme, close to the Rotonde fountain on place Général-de-Gaulle. Pick up the walking tour leaflet "In the Steps of Cézanne" here. Alternatively, stroll up cours Mirabeau to No. 55 (Cézanne's father's hat shop, now a linen store) and enter the Old Quarter through the tiny passage Agard. Return for a drink at the Café des Deux Garçons, No. 53 cours Mirabeau, where Cézanne met with other artists. Chic shops are in Quartier Mazarin, on the other side of the road.

5 Quartier Mazarin

It was here that 17th- and 18th-century Aix nobility built some of their finest town houses. Within this tranquil district of ornamental façades, small galleries and antiques shops, the discreet air of old money remains palpable.

6 Musée Granet

Housed in a former priory, built in 1671, this museum displays European art from the 16th to 19th centuries.

7 Granet XXe

The 16th-century Chapelle des Pénitents Blancs is the airy setting for the collection of Jean Planque, on long-term loan to the Granet. View over 300 works by artists such as Renoir, Monet, Van Gogh and Picasso.

8 Aix Market

The vast and colourful Aix market colonizes all the town's old squares on Tuesday, Thursday and Saturday mornings. From the place de Verdun via the place des Prêcheurs to the place de l'Hôtel de Ville, the streets come alive with stalls selling fresh produce, clothes and antiques.

9 Cathédrale St-Sauveur

This is the focal point of medieval Aix. Notable features are an octagonal, 5th-century baptistry, 12th-century carved cloisters (left) and the wonderful Buisson Ardent (Burning Bush) triptych painted in 1476 by Nicolas Froment.

10 Pavillon de Vendôme

Obliged to enter holy orders, local cardinal Louis de Mercoeur built this villa as a love-nest for his mistress in 1665. Its size, decorated façade and extensive gardens, however, suggest a somewhat open secret. It now houses contemporary art exhibitions.

Aix-en-Provence

NEED TO KNOW

MAP D4 ■ Office du Tourisme: 300 av Giuseppe Verdi; 04 42 16 11 61; www.aixenprovence tourism.com

Cathédrale St-Sauveur: 34 pl des Martyrs de la Résistance. **Open** 8am–6pm daily. Adm to cloisters

Musée Granet: pl St-Jean-de-Malte. **Open** Jun–Sep: 10am–7pm Tue–Sun; Oct–May: noon–6pm Tue–Sun. Closed 1 May. Adm €5

Atelier Cézanne: av Paul Cézanne; www.atelier-cezanne.com. **Open** 10am–12:30pm, 2–6pm (to 5pm Oct–Mar; 10am–6pm Jul, Aug). Closed 1–3 Jan, 1 May, 25 Dec, Sun Dec–Feb. Adm €6

Pavillon de Vendôme: 32 rue Célony. **Open** 10am–noon, 1:30–5:30pm Wed–Mon (to 6pm mid-Apr–mid-Oct); Closed Jan. Adm €3.50

Granet XXe: pl Jean Boyer. **Open** as Musée Granet. Adm €5

■ Aix is traditionally associated with *calissons* – yellow candied sweets made with almonds and fruit, and topped with a layer of icing.

TOP 10 ★ Vieux Nice

Foreign aristocrats and the rich and famous may have colonized other parts of the city, but Vieux Nice, just below the castle hill, belongs firmly to the Niçois, who claim it with Mediterranean gusto. Tiny streets throb with arm-waving commerce, and Baroque architecture slots into a warren of hanging washing, galleries, craft workshops and food stalls. The noise, mouthwatering aromas and vivid colours recall the city's long links with Italy – Nice became French as late as 1860. The lively atmosphere lasts well into the night in the neighbourhood's many trendy bars, restaurants and clubs.

1 Cathédrale Ste-Réparate

When the Dukes of Savoy ruled Nice they worshipped in this soaring, 17th-century church. It boasts a majestic polychrome cupola **(below)** and, within, the extravagance of the stuccoed Baroque decor is breathtaking.

3 Cours Saleya

The great square (or rather, oblong) **(right)** bursts into life every Tuesday to Sunday morning with the world-famous flower market. Come evening, bar and restaurant terraces buzz. On Monday mornings the flower market is replaced by an antiques and flea market. This is Vieux Nice's focal point, colourful and vigorous.

4 Palais Lascaris

Nice's most sumptuous 17th-century Baroque palace is now home to an exceptional museum of historic musical instruments.

5 Colline du Château

The castle that was once here was destroyed in 1706, but this hill still boasts splendid views. A botanical park covers the slope below.

7 Chapelle de la Miséricorde

If you see only one of Nice's Baroque churches, make sure it is this one. The splendour of the decoration **(below)** makes it one of the world's best examples of the style.

2 Rue St-François-de-Paule

This busy thoroughfare is home to two of the city's best-loved institutions: Maison Auer, a wonderful *chocolatière*, at No. 7, and Alziari, the olive and *"grand cru"* olive oil specialists, at No. 14.

6 Place St-François

This delightful square, overseen by an 18th-century clock tower and a Baroque palace, is the site of the fish and herb market, held around the dolphin fountain (open Tuesday to Sunday).

⑧ Opéra de Nice

This ornate building is home to ballet, classical music and opera. The theatre, designed by François Aune, a pupil of Gustave Eiffel, was reconstructed in 1885 following a fire which entirely destroyed the original. It was classified a *monument historique* in 1993.

⑨ Rue Pairolière

In this charming narrow street **(right)**, food shops spill over with *socca* (pancakes), salt cod and spicy meats, jostling for space amid Provençal fabrics and jewellery. Stroll through the crowds, soaking up the exciting mix of aromas, colours and Niçois accents.

BAROQUE CHURCHES

Vieux Nice is celebrated for its Baroque churches. In addition to those mentioned here, there are several others worth visiting: Ste-Rita (rue de la Poissonnerie); Gésu (rue Droite); St-Martin-St-Augustin (pl St-Augustin); St-François-de-Paule (rue St-François-de-Paule); St-Suaire (rue St-Suaire) and the Chapelle des Pénitents Rouges (rue Jules Gilly – Latin Mass every Sunday morning).

NEED TO KNOW

MAP H4 ▪ Office du Tourisme: 5 prom des Anglais; 08 92 70 74 07; en.nicetourism.com

Palais Lascaris: 15 rue Droite. **Open** 10am–6pm Wed–Mon (guided tours €6)

Chapelle de la Miséricorde: cours Saleya. **Open** 2:30–5pm Tue.

Cathédrale Ste- Réparate: pl Rossetti. **Open** 9am–noon, 2–6pm Tue–Sun (closed during Mass)

Opéra de Nice: 4–6 rue Saint-François de Paule. 04 92 17 40 40

▪ Save energy: take the free lift up Colline du Château from Quai des Etats-Unis.

▪ Vieux Nice is for pedestrians only; there's parking on pl Masséna.

⑩ Quartier du Malonat

Daily life courses through the tiny streets and squares, and beneath the washing and *trompe l'oeil* house decorations in the most authentic sector of Vieux Nice.

Vieux Nice

450 metres

Following pages Boats moored at Nice harbour

TOP 10 ⭐ St-Tropez

Within the space of a short stroll it is easy to see why this sun-soaked, congenial fishing village, with its pretty harbour, red-tiled houses and fabulous sandy beaches, seduced the painters, writers and Bohemians that made it famous. Despite all its hype as a world-famous tourism mecca of the rich and famous, "St-Trop" retains a good deal of its original charm – brightly painted fishing boats still moor in the Port de Pêche, although today they are increasingly outnumbered by gleaming yachts.

ARTISTIC MECCA

How did St-Tropez transform itself from undiscovered fishing village to holiday hotspot? Painter Paul Signac *(see p41)* must take half the blame: he arrived on his yacht in 1887, fell in love with the light and colour and decided to stay. Other painters followed, along with writers and would-be artists, attracted by warm weather and easy living. The film industry discovered the St-Trop scene in the 1950s, with the jet set following in its wake. Brigitte Bardot became its ultimate symbol in the Swinging Sixties and the place has never looked back.

1 Notre-Dame de l'Assomption

This ebullient Italian Baroque church, built in the early 1800s, contains a gilded bust of the town's patron saint, Tropez (or Torpès). According to legend, the Roman legionary converted to Christianity and was martyred by Emperor Nero. His body was pushed out to sea by the Romans before washing up where the town now stands.

2 Vieux Port

The quayside of the Old Port, quai Jean Jaurès **(above)**, is lined with leisure vessels year-round. In summer the waterside buzzes with artists, and pedestrians hoping to spot a celeb.

3 Citadel

The 17th-century ramparts surround a fort built to protect the village from Barbary corsairs. The citadel also houses the Musée Maritime.

St-Tropez and the church of Notre-Dame de l'Assomption

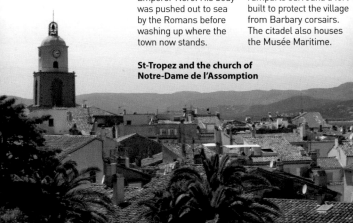

NEED TO KNOW

MAP F5 ■ Office du Tourisme: quai Jean Jaurès; 08 92 68 48 28;

Open daily; Jan–Mar, mid-Oct–Dec: 9:30am– 12:30pm, 2–6pm; Apr–Jun, Sep–mid-Oct: 9:30am– 12:30pm, 2–7pm; Jul, Aug: 9:30am–1:30pm, 3–7:30pm; www. sainttropeztourisme.com

Notre Dame de l'Assomption: rue de l'Eglise. **Open** 9:30am–noon Tue–Sun

■ Le Café on place des Lices, formerly the Café des Arts, is where St-Tropez's Bohemians hung out in the 1950s and 1960s heyday.

■ Visit the place des Lices on Tuesday or Saturday morning, when the square is crammed with enticing stalls selling flowers, fruit and antiques.

4 La Fontanette

The small La Fontanette beach, just east of La Ponche, is not as spectacular as those further afield, but is the only one within walking distance of the town and it is ideal for a cooling midday swim while you are exploring St-Tropez.

5 Place des Lices

This market square, immortalized by the painter Charles Camoin *(see p44)*, still has some of the atmosphere that he captured in his work. Crowded with open-air café tables, and shaded by plane trees, it is the perfect place in which to watch locals playing *pétanque* (boules).

6 Tour Suffren

Built in AD 880 by Guillaume I, Duke of Provence, this round tower overlooking the harbour was once part of a larger castle, the Château Suffren. The tower overlooks the fishing harbour where old boats are moored.

7 Musée de l'Annonciade

Close to the Vieux Port, a pretty 16th-century chapel has been wonderfully converted to house a world-class collection of paintings by famous artists connected with St-Tropez, including Bonnard, Derain, Dufy, Matisse, Rouault and Signac *(see p44)*.

8 Plages de Tahiti and Pampelonne

St-Tropez's beaches begin 4 km (2.5 miles) southeast of the town, on a long bay, the Anse de Pampelonne *(see p54)*. The 9-km (5-mile) sweep of sand is divided into smaller stretches, each with its own name.

9 Sentier des Douaniers

The "Customs Officers' Path" is part of a longer *sentier littoral* (coastal path) with spectacular views of the Côte d'Azur. The many tiny pebbly or sandy bays offer bathing opportunities away from the crowds. Energetic walkers can follow the path for 35 km (21 miles) to Cavalaire.

10 La Ponche

La Ponche (above) is the core of the original fishing village. With narrow streets, painted shutters and ochre walls, it looks much as it did before tourism arrived.

TOP 10 ★ The Camargue

Black bulls, white horses and pink flamingoes: these are the classic images of the Camargue delta where the Rhône meets the sea and France's only cowboys gallop across the flattest land in France. It's an 800 sq km (300 sq miles) zone of lagoons, salt flats and marshes; remote, romantic and rich in birdlife. Large stretches are protected and inaccessible, but open to all are the long evenings of gypsy music and wine as the sun sets on the horizon.

1 Abbaye de St-Gilles

This once-vast medieval abbey, in St-Gilles-du-Gard, was severely damaged in 1562. The carved façade (below), one of Provence's most beautiful, has survived intact.

2 The Salt Pans

The largest salt pans in Europe (below), in the southeast of the Camargue region, cover 100 sq km (40 sq miles) and produce 800,000 tonnes of salt a year. Reach the great mounds of salt via a little train at Salin d'Aigues Mortes.

3 Domaine de la Palissade

Visitors can explore the rich flora and fauna of this natural reserve either on foot (walks range from 30 minutes to 3 hours 30 minutes in duration) or, from April to October, in the saddle on a Camargue horse.

4 Musée de la Camargue

A converted sheep barn in Mas du Pont de Rousty is a fine setting for a little museum dealing with the interaction of man and nature in the Camargue, from the 19th century to today.

5 Les-Saintes-Maries-de-la-Mer

The tiny main street and bell towers of this old village teem with crowds and colour in summer, but its seaside charm remains intact. The May gypsy pilgrimage marks the legendary arrival of Mary Magdalene, Mary Jacoby, Mary Salome and their servant Sara, who is patron saint of gypsies.

6 Domaine de Méjanes

On the banks of Vaccarès lagoon, there are bull-game spectaculars on Sundays in August.

CAMARGUE BULLS AND HORSES

The liveliest of the lithe Camargue bulls are used in *course Camarguaise* bull-running games in village arenas and on the streets. Larger bulls are also raised for the *corridas* in Spain and southern France. The iconic Camargue horses only turn white as they reach adulthood. They are born almost black.

7 Parc Ornithologique du Pont-de-Gau

Next to the information centre is this splendid bird park **(below)**. Aviaries dotted around two acres of marshland house unusual birds that are very difficult to spot in the wild.

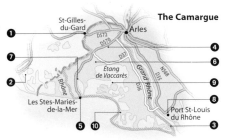

The Camargue

9 Parc Naturel Régional de Camargue

The HQ of the Camargue National Nature Reserve of the Vaccarès lagoon and surrounding area is in La Capelière, and has displays on ecosystems and climate. Nature trails and observation posts let you test out your new knowledge.

10 Plage de Beauduc

The "beach at the end of the world" **(below)** is the spot for wild camping and wild watersports in summer. Vehicles are not permitted here.

8 Port St-Louis du Rhône

This port town has an 18th-century tower, which once served as a look-out post. The tower now houses an ornithological museum and offers superb views of the salt marshes.

NEED TO KNOW

MAP A4 ■ Parc Ornithologique: Pont-de-Gau; www.parc ornithologique.com

Open daily (not 25 Dec)

Adm €7.50

Musée de la Camargue: Mas du Pont de Rousty; www. museedela camargue.com. **Open** Wed–Mon; Closed 1 Jan, 1 May, 25 Dec. Adm €5

Salin d'Aigues Mortes: 04 66 73 40 24. **Open** Mar–Oct. Adm €10 (museum and train)

Parc Naturel Régional de Camargue: La Capelière; 04 90 97 00 97. **Open** Apr–Sep: daily; Oct–Mar: Wed–Mon. Adm €3

Port-Saint-Louis-du-Rhône (Office du Tourisme): Tour Saint Louis–Quai Bonnardel, 04 42 86 01 21; www. portsaintlouis-tourisme.fr

Open times vary, check website for details

Domaine de la Palissade: Salin de Giraud; www. palissade.fr. **Open** Mar–Oct: daily; Nov & Feb: Wed–Mon. Adm €3, riding tours from €18

■ For the real Camargue experience be sure to visit a *manade* (farm).

TOP 10 ⭐ Vaison-la-Romaine

Vaison is a delightful town, boasting a magnificent array of Roman relics, including a graceful single-arched bridge that miraculously survived the devastating floods of the Ouvèze river in 1992. Founded by the Celtic Vocontii tribe, the town was named Vasio Vocontiorum after the Roman conquest, and for four centuries it flourished until the collapse of the empire, when the original site was abandoned for the safer precincts of the walled Ville Haute and its castle on the opposite bank of the Ouvèze. Between 1907 and 1955, a local abbot, Chanoine Sautel, excavated the Roman city.

1 Puymin
Named for the hill on which it stands, this district **(left)** was the most important part of the town in Roman times, containing the *praetorium* (court house), a theatre, temples and shops. There are also several well-preserved houses that can be explored. A broad road runs from the theatre to the main gate.

2 Maison des Messii
The House of the Messii must once have been home to one of the town's most important families. Columns and the foundations of an atrium, baths, a temple to household gods, a dining room and living rooms can all still be seen.

3 House with the Silver Bust
Named after a statue found here and now on show in the museum, the ruins of this once grand, mosaic-floored villa are enhanced by copies of statues found here and elsewhere on the site.

4 House with the Dolphin
The House with the Dolphin was named after the marble statue of Cupid riding a dolphin found here, now in the museum. The villa once had a façade supported by 18 columns.

5 Musée Théo Desplans
A muscular, life-size marble nude of the Emperor Hadrian **(left)**, a statue of his empress Sabina, a gorgeous silver bust found at the Villasse site, and a six-seater public latrine are among the more interesting archaeological finds in this excellent small museum.

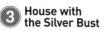

6 Portico of Pompey
This impressive portico, built by the family of Caesar's great rival Pompey, is a huge, 65-m (210-ft) array of columns, which originally surrounded an inner garden. Built around AD 20, it was demolished during the 5th century. Copies of statues that originally stood on the site now grace the niches – the originals are preserved in the nearby museum.

7 Théâtre Antique

The 1st-century AD theatre **(below)** is a dazzling display of Roman building skill, with 34 semi-circular rows of stone benches, seating up to 7,000 spectators, rising to a columned portico.

8 Nymphaeum

The Nymphaeum was a rectangular sacred pool with a fountain, which was covered by a roof supported by four columns. Traces of the building still remain, as does the sacred spring which provided the water supply. It now forms an elegant backdrop to an open-air theatre.

9 Haute Ville and the Pont Romain

Vaison's 2,000-year-old Roman bridge connects the upper town on the south bank with the north bank of the Ouvèze. The prettily restored old quarter **(below)**, with its 17th-century town houses, courtyards and fountains, is ringed by ramparts and entered through a massive, 14th-century stone gateway.

10 Château

At the highest point of the old town stands a dramatic, part-ruined castle **(above)**, built in 1160 by the Count of Toulouse. Three main wings and a formidable keep tower surround an inner courtyard.

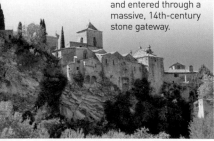

TOP 10 ⭐ Abbaye Notre-Dame de Sénanque

Surrounded by the lavender fields of the Luberon, this lovely abbey exudes tranquillity, but its past was anything but peaceful. Founded in 1148, Sénanque's golden age was the 13th century, but in 1544 it was torched by heretic Vaudois *(see p126)*, in 1580 it was stricken by the plague, and by the 17th century only two monks were left. The French Revolution and the anti-monastic laws of the 19th century were equally harsh but, since the 1970s, the abbey's fortunes have been restored, and ten monks are now in permanent residence here.

1 Apse
The three windows of the raised, semi-circular apse symbolize the Holy Trinity.

2 Nave and Transept
The barrel-vaulted nave **(below)** and aisles of Sénanque are five bays long, and three stone steps lead from the nave to the square crossing, with its eight-sided dome.

4 Abbey Shop
The Cistercians believe in work as well as prayer, and the fruits of their labours are here. This shop sells their own lavender essential oil and honey from their hives, and books and products made in other convents and monasteries across France.

5 Channels
The Cistercians came to this plateau seeking isolation, and built their abbey next to the region's only river, the Senancole. They channelled the water to flow through and under the abbey, providing sanitation and irrigation for the gardens.

3 Cloister
The dove-grey limestone columns of the cloister **(right)**, decorated with delicate carvings of leaves, flowers and vines, are superb works of craftsmanship, dating from between 1180 and 1220.

6 Dormitory

The dormitory is a huge, vaulted space, paved with flagstones. Arched windows **(left)** at regular intervals along its walls and two large, circular windows at each end make this otherwise austere room feel pleasantly light and airy.

7 Tomb of the Seigneur de Venasque

In one corner of the east arm of the transept is the only non-Cistercian element of the church – a lovely Gothic tomb marks the burial place of Geoffroy, the 13th-century Lord of Venasque and at one time the abbey's benefactor.

8 Lavender Fields

The abbey of Notre-Dame de Sénanque is surrounded by fields of lavender **(left)** which make a spectacular setting for the buildings in the summer.

9 Calefactory

The calefactory and scriptorium reflects St Bernard's injunctions against luxury: with two fireplaces, this was the only heated room in the monastery, which enabled monks to read without their hands freezing.

10 Chapterhouse

The walls of the square chapterhouse, are lined with stone seats **(above)**. Here the monks sat each day to hear the abbot read a chapter from the Rule of St Benedict or a sermon from the Bible.

ST BERNARD AND THE CISTERCIANS

With their complete lack of decoration or comfort, Provence's most outstanding Romanesque monasteries, Sénanque, Silvacane (see p82) and Le Thoronet (see p88), reflect the austere ideals of the Cistercian order, founded in 1098 by St Bernard, abbot of Clairvaux in north-east France. Rejecting the ostentation and luxury of the powerful Benedictine order, St Bernard advocated a rigorous and pure monastic life within simple, yet graceful and harmonious buildings.

NEED TO KNOW

MAP C3 ■ 04 90 72 05 86 ■ www.senaque.fr ■ Spiritual retreats: email frere.hotelier@senanque.fr

Open non-guided visits: 9:45–11am Mon–Sat; guided tours (in French): book online at least 48 hours ahead; arrive 10 mins before tour. Mass: 8:30am Mon, 11:45am Tue–Sat, 10am Sun & bank hols. Closed mid-Nov–Jan (am), Ascension (sixth Sun after Easter), 15 Aug, 1 Nov, during snow.

Adm: €7:50 (tours)

■ Silence and respectful dress are requested.

■ The most striking approach to Sénanque is from Gordes, with a panorama of the abbey as the road descends into the craggy valley in which Sénanque stands.

TOP 10 ⭐ Casino de Monte Carlo

Monte Carlo's magnificent *belle époque* casino was built in 1863 by Charles Garnier, architect of the Paris opera house. With its commanding position and stunning views, it is impressive enough from the outside. But within it is truly dazzling: a veritable temple to luck, luxury and ostentatious self-indulgence, haunted by the phantoms of aristocratic gamblers including the Prince of Wales (later King Edward VII), Grand Duke Nicholas of Russia and many more. The stage of the Salle Garnier attracted artistic talents such as the great ballet choreographers Diaghilev and Nijinsky. Modern slot machines and video poker screens look decidedly out of place amid these grand surroundings.

NEED TO KNOW

MAP H3 ■ Pl du Casino, Monte Carlo, Monaco
■ 00 377 98 06 21 21
■ www.casinomonte carlo.com

Games rooms for viewing only: **Open** 9am–noon daily. Adm €10

Games rooms for gambling: **Open** 2pm–late daily. Adm €10

■ If you want to gamble, ignore the roulette wheel and head straight for the blackjack table. It's the only game where the odds – ever so slightly – favour the player rather than the casino.

■ A passport or ID card is required to gamble, and jacket and tie are required in the private lounges.

Salle Europe ①

The opulent Salle Europe is lit by eight huge chandeliers of glittering Bohemian crystal **(right)**. But even they don't shine as brightly as the 80 slot machines here.

② Salle Garnier

Named after the casino's architect, this opera house is lavishly decked out in red and gold, its walls adorned with frescoes and encrusted with gilded bas-reliefs.

③ Salle Blanche

The wall painting in the White Room lounge-bar **(above)**, *Graces of Florence*, depicts three muses said to represent 19th-century courtesans, Cleo de Merode, Liane de Pougy and Otero.

6 Atrium

Paved in marble, the vast entrance hall is surrounded by 28 Ionic columns. The atrium links the casino with the Salle Garnier, and its grandeur gives a hint of what awaits within.

7 Salles Privées

The Salle Médecin and Salle Touzet, once the casino's private rooms, are now open to all who pay a small charge in addition to the admission fee. High rollers gather round the games tables in elegant surroundings of gilded mahogany.

8 Café de Paris

King Edward VII was a regular customer to the *belle époque* café in front of the casino, first known as the Café Divan. In the 1930s, while retaining its original façade, it was transformed into an Art Deco triumph and was lovingly renovated again in 1988 *(see p110)*.

4 Casino Café de Paris

Replacing the casino's former smoking room, this up-to-the-minute games room is situated inside the Café de Paris. It features modern machines and tables, and is reminiscent of Las Vegas.

9 Renaissance Hall

This large room filled with roulette tables and slot machines is the casino's main gaming room. Its *belle époque* finery imitates the high style of the Italian Renaissance.

Jardins de Casino 5

Opposite the casino are the magnificent flower gardens, immaculate lawns, terraces and lily pools of the Casino Gardens **(right)**, sloping up towards Monaco's most exclusive shopping area *(see p107)*.

THE MAN WHO BROKE THE BANK

Many visitors to the casino still follow the superstitious tradition of stroking the knee of the horse – part of an equestrian statue of Louis XIV – in the foyer of the Hôtel de Paris, to bring luck. Luckiest of all was Charles Wells, who, in 1891, raked in one million gold francs in a three-day winning streak, then won three million more on a second visit. The event inspired the song "The Man Who Broke the Bank at Monte Carlo". But his luck failed in the end and, on a third visit, the casino cleaned him out.

10 Salle des Ameriques

This lavishly renovated, ornate red and gold room **(above)** is dedicated to American table games, including craps, blackjack, 21 and American-style roulette.

The Top 10 of Everything

Magnificent 15th-century frescoes in Notre-Dame des Fontaines, La Brigue

🔟 Moments in History

Carvings in the Vallée des Merveilles

1 Early Settlers

Rock carvings found in the Grotte d'Observatoire in Monaco and paintings in the Grotte Cosquer near Marseille date from 350,000 BC. Between 2500 and 2000 BC, dwellers in the Vallée des Merveilles *(see p114)* left behind over 10,000 carvings of beasts and figures.

2 Foundation of Aix

In 123 BC, Greeks from Phocaea (modern Turkey), who had settled in Marseille since 600 BC, asked Rome for help against the invading Celtic tribes. After defeating the Celts, the Romans founded the town of Aquae Sextia (Aix-en-Provence) *(see pp18–19)*.

Roman mosaic found in Aix-en-Provence

3 Advent of Christianity

In AD 40 St Honorat brought Christianity to Provence, founding the first monastery on Île de Lérins. Camarguais legend, however, claims that Christianity was introduced to Provence by Mary Magdalene herself *(see p39)*.

4 Franks and Saracens

With the fall of the Roman Empire in AD 476 Provence was pillaged by barbarians, eventually coming under the rule of the Franks. From the 8th century the coasts were harried by Moorish pirates who gave their name to the Massif des Maures. They were finally defeated in 974 by Guillaume le Libérateur, Count of Arles.

5 Dawn of a Dynasty

In 1297 François Grimaldi, a supporter of the papacy in the Guelph-Ghibelline feuds which beset 13th-century Italy, seized Monaco and its castle to found the dynasty that still rules there today.

6 The Avignon Papacy

Pope Clement V relocated to Avignon in 1309 to escape strife-torn Rome, the first of a succession of nine French pontiffs who were to reside in the Provençal town. In 1348 Clement VI bought the city and Avignon remained the seat of the papacy until 1377 *(see pp12–13)*.

Pope Clement V at Avignon

King René, ruler of Provence

7 Union with France
In 1486 King René of Naples, the last of the Anjou dynasty who ruled Provence from 1246, died without issue, and most of the region became part of France. Nice and the Alpes Maritimes, however, remained part of the Kingdom of Savoy, before finally passing to France in 1860.

8 Plague and War
In the second half of the 16th century religious strife erupted in the Luberon between reforming Vaudois and Huguenot factions and conservative Catholics. The plague of 1580 added to the region's woes.

9 La Marseillaise
When the French Revolution erupted in July 1789, the citizens of Marseille were among its staunchest supporters, marching to a tune that became known as La Marseillaise, now France's national anthem.

10 Resistance and Liberation
After the Nazi invasion of 1940, Provence was ruled by the collaborationist Vichy government, until it was occupied by Germany in 1942. Guerrilla fighters in the *maquis* (scrubland) resisted the Occupation. On 15 August 1944, Allied troops landed, liberating Provence after two weeks of fighting.

TOP 10 FIGURES IN HISTORY

1 Julius Caesar
Caesar besieged Marseille after its citizens sided with his biggest political rival Pompey in 49 BC.

2 François Grimaldi
Grimaldi disguised his troop of soldiers as monks in order to seize control of Monaco in 1297.

3 The Anti-Pope
When the papacy returned to Rome, French cardinals elected Robert de Genève as Pope Clement VII, creating a split in the Church until 1417.

4 Petrarch
The renowned Italian Renaissance poet (1304–74), who spent much of his early life in Avignon, was a critic of the ostentatious French papacy.

5 Nostradamus
Born in St-Rémy-de-Provence, the scholar (1503–66) published his book of prophecies in 1555.

6 Napoleon Bonaparte
Bonaparte landed at Golfe-Juan on 1 March 1815 to regain his empire, only to be defeated at Waterloo.

7 Louis-Auguste Blanqui
Born in Puget-Théniers in 1805, the socialist was one of the leaders of the revolutionary Paris Commune of 1871.

8 Jacques Cousteau
Toulon-based naval officer Cousteau perfected the aqualung in the 1940s, pioneering the sport of scuba diving.

9 Antoine de St-Exupéry
The aircraft of the French author and pilot vanished in 1944 while on a reconnaissance flight over Provence.

10 Brigitte Bardot
Sex icon and film star Bardot became the symbol of St-Tropez in the 1960s.

Brigitte Bardot

TOP 10 Provençal Legends

Red rocky outcrop in Roussillon

1 Roussillon

The red cliffs of Roussillon are not coloured by accident. In medieval times the local lord's wife, Sirmonde, fell in love with a troubadour. The lord had him killed and Sirmonde threw herself off a cliff, staining the rocks with her blood *(see p129)*.

2 Man in the Iron Mask

Who was the Man in the Iron Mask? Louis XIV's troublesome brother? A meddling royal priest? No one knows. Certainly, he was dangerous enough to be clamped in a mask and locked away in Château d'If from 1687. You may visit the island fort and see his cell *(see p77)*.

3 Pont d'Avignon

In 1177 a shepherd boy named Bénézet received orders from God that a bridge should be built across the Rhône. Avignon people were sceptical, so the lad picked up a rock that 30 strong men couldn't shift and carried it to where Pont St-Bénézet was to begin *(see p128)*.

4 Avignon's Hidden Treasure

Pope John XXII was rumoured to be an alchemist, who used magic to win his election. He had an amulet to detect poison (supposedly because other churchmen kept trying to kill him) and made enough gold to fill an underground room. When Benedict XIII, the last Avignon anti-pope, was forced to flee, he walled it up. It has never been found *(see pp12–13)*.

5 St Maximin-la-Ste-Baume

After reputedly landing in Provence, Mary Magdalene spread the Christian word, before spending her last years praying in a cave in the Ste-Baume mountains. Her remains were discovered in the 13th century and may be seen in a reliquary in the Gothic basilica *(see p88)*.

6 Cathérine Ségurane, Nice

Washerwoman Cathérine led Niçois resistance against the Turkish fleet that besieged the city in 1543. She knocked out the Turkish standard-bearer with her washboard, before lifting her skirts and putting the rest of the Turks to flight. The battle was eventually lost, but Cathérine has a statue in Vieux Nice *(see pp20–21)*.

The famous Pont d'Avignon

⑦ Les Pénitents des Mées

In AD 800 a group of monks ogled female Saracen prisoners being led to the Durance river and were turned to stone as punishment. There they remain – a 2 km (1 mile) line of rocks, some 100 m (300 ft) high, looking like repentant monks with their cowls up *(see p122)*.

Les Pénitents des Mées

⑧ Saintes-Maries-de-la-Mer

After being set adrift in a boat from Palestine, Mary Jacoby (sister of the Virgin Mary), Mary Magdalene, Mary Salome, Lazarus and a servant girl, Sara, landed on the Provençal coast. They were the first Christians in Gaul. The "relics" of Jacoby and Salome are found in the town's church, as are those of Sara, patron saint of gypsies *(see p84)*.

⑨ Lost "City of God"

The Latin inscription on a rock near St-Geniez indicates the site of a 5th-century "Theopolis", or City of God Christian centre. No other trace has ever been found. However, phenomena here, including strange lights and odd weather, add to the mystery.

⑩ La Tarasque, Tarascon

The Tarasque, a dragon-like beast, terrorized Tarascon in the 1st century AD, until St Martha sprinkled it with holy water. The Tarasque remains central to the town's lively June festival *(see p81)*.

TOP 10 TRADITIONS

1 Midnight Mass, Christmas Eve
Pastoral memories mix with Christian ritual, as live lambs join in the Mass.

2 Thirteen Christmas Desserts
Symbolizing Christ and the Apostles, the climax of the Christmas Eve meal includes dried fruit and griddle cakes.

3 Nativity Scenes
Depictions of Christ's birth mix biblical characters with traditional terracotta *santon* figures of Provençal villagers.

4 Fête de la St-Jean
MAP B2 ▪ 23 Jun
In Valréas, a medieval-style costumed parade attends to the election of a boy to "protect" the town.

5 Les Tripettes, Barjols
MAP E4 ▪ 2nd weekend Jan
Celebrates St Marcel with a bull sacrifice, village-wide distribution of tripe, and singing and dancing.

6 Fête de la Tarasque, Tarascon
MAP B3 ▪ Last weekend Jun
The fearsome Tarasque "reappears" each year to terrify revellers.

7 Fête de la Transhumance, Riez
MAP E3 ▪ Sun, mid-Jun
Sheep cross the village to an upland pasture, giving rise to festivities.

8 Fête de la Lavande, Sault
MAP C2 ▪ 15 Aug
The heartland of lavender *(see p127)* celebrates the year's harvest.

9 Fête des Mimosas, Bormes-les-Mimosas
MAP E5 ▪ Mid-Feb
Festivities amid the flowers *(see p88)*.

10 Fête des Vins, Bandol
MAP D5 ▪ 1st Sun, Dec
This acclaimed wine district celebrates the completion of its latest vintage.

Provençal nativity scene

TOP 10 Painters in Provence

Van Gogh's *The Red Vineyard Near Arles* (1888)

1 Vincent van Gogh
The Dutch Post-Impressionist created hundreds of his most vivid, powerful landscapes and self-portraits during his few years in Arles and St-Rémy. The sunshine of Provence is said to have changed the way Van Gogh (1854–90) saw light and colour.

2 Yves Klein
Born in Iceland, Klein (1928–62) became one of the leading lights of the Nice School of New Realists, who aimed to create art from everyday materials. His *Anthropométries*, in Nice's Musée d'Art Moderne et d'Art Contemporain (see p95), was created by three nude women, covered in his signature blue paint, rolling over a huge white canvas.

3 Paul Cézanne
Born in Aix, where he lived most of his life, Cézanne (1839–1906) painted hundreds of oil and watercolour scenes of his home town and the nearby Mont Sainte-Victoire (see pp18–19) in his characteristic Post-Impressionist style. Better than any other painter, he captures the soul of Provence.

4 Marc Chagall
The Russian-born painter (1887–1985) moved to St-Paul-de-Vence in 1949. His light-filled work was often inspired by biblical themes. Canvases from his Biblical Message series of paintings are in the Musée National Marc Chagall in Nice (see p97).

5 Fernand Léger
Léger (1881–1955) is known for his strong Cubist paintings and his love of bold lines and pure primary colours. First a figurative painter, he worked in the Cubist style before returning to painting that seems to echo poster or graphic art.

Cezanne's *François Zola Dam* (1877–8)

6 Raoul Dufy

Dufy (1877–1955) embodies the values of the Fauvist school, with its revolutionary use of bright, intense colour. He found Nice the perfect background for his vivid work.

7 Henri Matisse

Matisse (1869–1954) lived in Nice from 1917 until his death. His earlier works were inspired by the vivid light and colours of the Riviera. During World War II he retreated to Vence, where he designed the unique Chapelle du Rosaire, including its wonderful Stations of the Cross, vestments and furnishings (see p47).

8 Paul Signac

A master of the Pointillist style, Signac (1863–1935) came to St-Tropez in 1892. He found, in the sparkle of sun on sea, the perfect subject for Pointillism's technique of using a myriad of tiny rainbow dots to depict swathes or blocks of colour.

Signac's *Antibes, the Pink Cloud* (1916)

9 Pablo Picasso

Picasso (1881–1973) was influenced by the sights and colours of Provence, where he lived in exile from his native Spain for much of his life. He learned to make ceramics from the potters of Vallauris and helped revive the craft (see p108).

10 Paul Guigou

This realist painter (1834–71) illustrated the landscapes of his native Vaucluse. Among his best-known works is *Deux Lavandières devant la Sainte-Victoire*, in the Musée Grobet-Labadié in Marseille (see p76).

TOP 10 WRITERS IN PROVENCE

Albert Camus

1 Frédéric Mistral
This Nobel Prize-winner (1830–1914) wrote epic poems based on local lore.

2 Alexandre Dumas
Dumas (1802–70) used the Château d'If (see p77) as the grim backdrop to *The Count of Monte Cristo* (1845).

3 Victor Hugo
Hugo (1802–85) set the early chapters of his epic novel *Les Misérables* (1862) in the area around Digne-les-Bains.

4 Albert Camus
This French author and existentialist (1913–60) wrote his respected autobiography at Lourmarin.

5 Alphonse Daudet
Daudet (1849–97) is best remembered for *Tartarin de Tarascon*, the popular tale of a Provençal bumpkin.

6 Graham Greene
The English novelist (1914–91) retired to Nice, where he wrote *J'Accuse – the Dark Side of Nice* (1982).

7 F Scott Fitzgerald
The US writer (1896–1940) stayed at Juan-les-Pins in 1926 while he wrote his novel *Tender is the Night*.

8 Edith Wharton
Wharton (1862–1937) spent winters at her villa in Hyères, where she finished *The Age of Innocence*, the first book by a woman to win the Pulitzer Prize.

9 Marcel Pagnol
The famous French author and film director (1895–1974) wrote *L'Eau des Collines* (1963), later filmed as *Jean de Florette* and *Manon des Sources*.

10 Colette
Colette (1873–1954) wrote charmingly of St-Tropez in *La Naissance du Jour* ("break of day") published in 1928.

📖10 Roman Sights

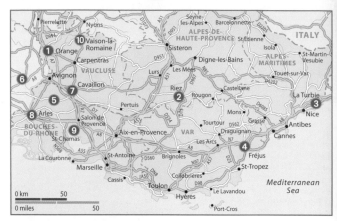

Théâtre Antique d'Orange

1 Théâtre Antique d'Orange

One of the best-preserved theatres from the Roman empire, built during the reign of Augustus (c.27–25 BC), is the highlight of the Parc de la Colline St-Eutrope. A triumphal arch decorated with relief carvings commemorates Julius Caesar's victories over Gaul (see p125).

2 Temple of Apollo, Riez
MAP E3

The four Corinthian columns of the 1st-century-AD temple to Apollo, standing tall and alone among fields just outside Riez on the Valensole plateau, are all that remain of the once prosperous Roman settlement of Reia Apollinaris. Eight ancient

pillars, perhaps scavenged from another Roman building, are now in the early Christian church nearby, which dates from the 4th or 5th century BC and is one of the oldest surviving churches in France.

3 La Trophée des Alpes, La Turbie

This majestic Roman monument, built from local white stone, was erected in 6 BC to mark the boundary between Italy and Gaul and to honour Augustus's Gallic conquests. Towering over the small village of La Turbie, high above Monte Carlo, with breathtaking views over the Riviera, it still has the power to impress (see p112).

4 Les Arènes de Fréjus
MAP F4 ■ Rue H Vadon
■ Open Apr–Sep: 9:30am–12:30pm, 2–6pm Tue–Sun; Oct–Mar: 9:30am–noon, 2–4:30pm Tue–Sat
■ Closed public hols ■ Adm

Like other large Roman arenas in Provence, the amphitheatre at Fréjus (see p87), which can seat up to 10,000 people, is still used regularly for bull-fights and classical music concerts. It was originally built in the 1st and 2nd centuries AD. Nearby are parts of the original Roman wall.

Glanum, near St-Rémy

5 Les Antiques de Glanum

Twin temples, a Roman forum, baths and a fortified gate can be seen at Glanum, near St-Rémy, which also reveals traces of a 4th-century Greek settlement. A triumphal arch (10 BC) marks Gallic victories *(see p83)*.

6 Pont du Gard
MAP A3

The Romans considered this 49-m-(160-ft-) high three-tiered bridge to be clear testimony to their empire's greatness. The top tier was part of an aqueduct that supplied Nîmes with water for up to 500 years. Constructed in the 1st century AD from dressed stone blocks without mortar, the bridge is an incredible 275 m (900 ft) long and represents an astonishing feat of engineering.

7 Arc de Triomphe, Cavaillon
MAP C3

This twin-arched triumphal gate, lavishly adorned with carved vines and dramatic Corinthian columns, was built during the reign of the Emperor Augustus, in the 1st century AD. There are other interesting Roman finds in the town's archaeological museum.

8 Arles

Remnants of Provence's most important Roman settlement can still be seen in numerous spots around this lovely town *(see pp16–17)*.

9 Pont Flavien, St-Chamas

One of the best-preserved Roman bridges in France, Pont Flavien was built in a single arch over the River Touloubre in the 1st century AD, as part of Emperor Augustus's Via Julia Augusta, which linked Piacenzia (Palantia) in Italy to Arles. Many Roman bridges had triumphal arches at either end, but this is the only one with arches that have survived intact *(see p84)*.

10 Vaison-la-Romaine

Another Roman gem, discovered in 1907 *(see pp28–9)*.

Magnificent Pont du Gard, spanning the Gardon river

🔟 Art Galleries

Exterior of the Musée National Marc Chagall, Nice

① Musée National Marc Chagall, Nice

One of the jewels of Provence, this museum houses the world's largest collection of works by Marc Chagall, including 17 canvases from his Biblical Message series *(see p97)*.

② Musée Fernand Léger, Biot

Mosaics in primary colours, carried out to Léger's own design, identify this strikingly modern museum. The Cubist painter planned to build a studio here just before his death in 1955, and the museum on the site exhibits more than 400 of his works *(see p113)*.

③ Musée de l'Annonciade, St-Tropez

MAP F5 ■ Pl Grammont, Vieux Port ■ Open 10am–1pm, 2–6pm Wed–Mon ■ Closed 1 Jan, Ascension (sixth Sun after Easter), 1 May, 17 May, Nov, 25 Dec ■ Adm

This serene former chapel houses an interesting art collection. Opened in 1955, it boasts works by Pierre Bonnard, Raoul Dufy, Paul Signac and Charles Camoin, whose *St-Tropez, la place des Lices et le Café des Arts* (1925) is one of the most famous images of the town *(see p25)*.

④ Musée Bonnard, Le Cannet

MAP G4 ■ 16 bd Sadi Carnot ■ Open 10am–6pm Tue–Sun (Jul & Aug: to 8pm) ■ Adm

Pierre Bonnard spent most of 1926–47 in Le Cannet, and this museum, in a *belle époque* villa, displays some of his finest canvases. Links with the Musée d'Orsay in Paris bring frequent special exhibitions.

⑤ Fondation Maeght, St-Paul-de-Vence

This small museum has a world-class array of modern art, including paintings by Léger, Bonnard and Chagall, sculpture by Miró and a mosaic pool by Braque *(see p115)*.

⑥ Musée d'Art Moderne et d'Art Contemporain (MAMAC), Nice

A dazzling work of contemporary architecture in its own right, with marble-faced towers and glass corridors, the contemporary art museum contains works by some of the 20th century's greatest avant-garde artists *(see p95)*.

⑦ Musée Matisse, Nice

Founded in 1963, nine years after the painter's death, the Musée Matisse is located in the 17th-century Villa des Arènes. There are sketches, paintings and bronze sculpture by Matisse, as well as some of his personal effects *(see p95)*.

The façade of the Musée Matisse, Nice

Musée du Bastion, Menton

⑧ Musée du Bastion and Musée Jean Cocteau, Menton

MAP H3 ■ Musée du Bastion: Quai Napoleon III; Musée Cocteau: 2 Quai de Monleon ■ Open 10am–6pm Wed–Mon (Jul, Aug: to 10pm Fri) for both museums ■ Closed public hols ■ Adm

The multi-talented Jean Cocteau, a playwright, author and film director, converted this 17th-century fort into his personal museum. Nearby, the Musée Cocteau houses 1,800 pieces donated by the art enthusiast and Cocteau devotee Séverin Wunderman.

Renoir's studio, Cagnes-sur-Mer

⑨ Musée Renoir, Cagnes-sur-Mer

Auguste Renoir's house at Les Collettes, where the painter came in hope that the climate would cure his rheumatism, houses 11 of his paintings. The house is surrounded by beautiful olive groves (see p105).

⑩ Musée Picasso, Antibes

Housed in the Château Grimaldi, used as a studio by Picasso in 1946, the museum contains more than 50 of his paintings, sketches, prints and ceramics, as well as works by Léger and Miró (see p104).

TOP 10 MASTERPIECES OF PROVENCE

L'Orage by Paul Signac

1 Café du Soir
Vincent van Gogh painted more than 300 canvases in the town of Arles (see pp16–17). Café du Soir (1888) is perhaps one of the best known.

2 La Joie de Vivre
This 1946 work is one of Picasso's most important from his Antibes period.

3 La Partie de Campagne
Fernand Léger overlays bold colours on bold, comic-book outlines in this esteemed 1954 painting.

4 Nu Bleu IV
The 1952 work is among the best known of Matisse's famous blue paper cut-outs series.

5 Coronation of the Virgin
Enguerrand Quarton's Renaissance painting of 1453 is the masterpiece of the French Avignon school.

6 L'Orage
Pointillist Paul Signac's 1895 work depicts St-Tropez harbour.

7 La Montagne Sainte-Victoire au Grand Pin
This 1887 painting is one of Cézanne's most renowned images of the Provence mountain (see p18).

8 The Burning Bush
Nicolas Froment's 1476 triptych in the Cathédrale de St-Saveur at Aix (see p19) was commissioned by Provence's last king, René.

9 Jetée Promenade à Nice
Portraying an evening stroll on the esplanade, the 1928 work is Dufy at his colourful best.

10 Venus Victrix
One of Renoir's most magnificent bronzes (1914) stands amid the olive groves at Les Collettes.

🔟 Places of Worship

Frescoed interior of Notre-Dame des Fontaines

1 Notre-Dame des Fontaines, La Brigue

MAP H2 ▪ Rue Notre-Dame des Fontaines ▪ Open mid-Apr–mid-Oct: 10am–12:30pm, 2–5:30pm ▪ Closed Tue, Thu pm ▪ Adm

This chapel, 4 km (2.5 miles) from La Brigue, is covered with remarkable frescoes by Giovanni Canavesio and Giovanni Baleison, dating from 1492.

2 Chapelle des Pénitents Blancs, Les-Baux-de-Provence

MAP B4 ▪ Open 10am–5pm daily

Frescoes in this simple chapel, painted in 1974 by local artist Yves Brayer, depict a typical Provençal nativity scene with shepherds. More of Brayer's work can be seen in the nearby museum (see p82).

3 Notre-Dame-du-Puy, Grasse

MAP G4 ▪ 8 pl du Petit Puy ▪ Open 9am–noon, 1–5pm daily (Jul–Sep: 10am–noon, 1–6pm) ▪ DA

Fragonard's *Christ Washing the Disciples' Feet* is the main reason for visiting this 13th-century church. It also contains three magnificent religious works by Rubens, all painted in 1601: *The Crown of Thorns*, *The Crucifixion of Christ* and *The Deposition of St Helena*.

4 Église St-Trophime, Arles

MAP B4 ▪ Pl de la République ▪ Open mid-Apr–Sep: 8am–noon, 2–7pm Mon–Sat, 9am–1pm, 3–7pm Sun; Oct–mid-Apr: 8am–noon, 2–6pm daily ▪ Closed 1 Jan, 1 May, 1 Nov, 25 Dec ▪ Adm: cloister

This is one of the most attractive of all Provençal churches. It's also one of the oldest – a church stood here as early as AD 450. In the 11th century the church was rebuilt and dedicated to St Trophime (see p16).

Carvings on the Église St-Trophime

5 Notre-Dame de Nazareth, Vaison-la-Romaine

MAP C2 ▪ Esplanade Yves Meffre ▪ Open Jun–Sep: 9am–6pm daily; other times call 04 90 36 50 48 ▪ DA

This evocative 6th-century cathedral has a superb arcaded apse and 12th-century cloister.

6 Église de Notre-Dame, Les-Saintes-Maries-de-la-Mer

The bell tower of this fortified church is a Camargue landmark. The church has lent its name to the capital of the region, and its sturdy walls offered refuge from raiders. The most colourful sight within is a carved boat with statues of the Virgin and Mary Magdalene and a statue of St Sara in the crypt. The gypsy pilgrimage in May marks the legendary arrival of Mary Magdalene by boat (see p26).

5 Cathédrale, Fréjus

Constructed in the pink stone typical of Fréjus, the 13th-century cathedral has a beautiful Renaissance doorway. Its interior is dominated by superb pointed arches, and the cloister ceiling, with its scenes of the Apocalypse, is unique (see p87).

8 Notre-Dame de l'Assomption, Puget-Théniers

MAP G3 ■ Open 8am–6pm daily

Built by the Knights Templar, the 13th-century parish church of this mountain village has a lovely altarpiece, *Notre Dame de Secours* (1525), by Antoine Ronzen of the Passion carried out by Flemish craftsmen, possibly working with architect and sculptor Matthieu d'Anvers.

9 Abbaye de Montmajour

The extraordinary abbey of Montmajour was built on a rocky island amid the Rhône marshes. It was an important pilgrimage site and became wealthy from selling pardons for sins. The cloister is decorated with mythical and biblical scenes (see p82).

The stunning Abbaye de Montmajour

10 Chapelle du Rosaire de Vence

MAP G4 ■ Open 2–5:30pm Mon, Wed, Sat; 10–11:30am, 2–5:30pm Tue, Thu (also Fri in Jul & Aug); Mass 10am Sun, followed by guided tour ■ Closed mid-Nov–mid-Dec ■ DA ■ Adm

The dazzling white interior walls of this little chapel are adorned with black line drawings of the Stations of the Cross. They are unmistakably the work of Henri Matisse (see p41), who designed this building in 1949.

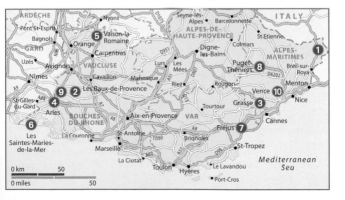

🔟 Provence Villages

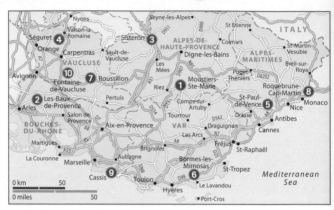

1 Moustiers-Ste-Marie

At the entrance to the Verdon gorges (see pp14–15), Moustiers hangs like a pendant from the rock face soaring above (see p14). The glorious tangle of vaulted streets and tiny squares are divided by rushing streams. High above, tucked against the rocks, is the Notre-Dame-de-Beauvoir chapel (see p119). The village is also celebrated for its pottery.

2 Les-Baux-de-Provence

Emerging dramatically from its crag on the edge of the Alpilles hills, Les-Baux was home to one of the finest courts in medieval Provence. Abandoned for centuries, the ruined castle and labyrinthine streets now throb with summer tourists. But the site remains majestic, the atmosphere lively and the views over mountains and plains quite breathtaking (see p82).

3 Sisteron

At the northern gateway to Provence, Sisteron's minuscule vaulted streets and unexpected staircases climb the vast sentinel rock overlooking the Durance river. It's a harsh setting for a village with a strong past. Up top, the 14th-century citadel was all but impregnable and now affords unbeatable views over the rugged landscape (see p120).

Sisteron, overlooking the Durance

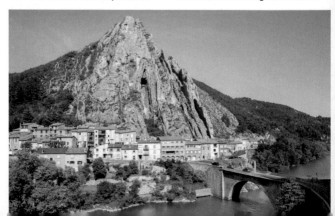

Cobbled street in Séguret

the red-and-gold earth into cliffs, canyons and weird formations. Villagers have applied the local product to their houses, to enchanting effect (see p129).

8 Roquebrune-Cap-Martin
A winning partnership of the sort only found on the Côte d'Azur. Beneath Roquebrune are the grandiose *belle époque* villas of the super-rich on the Cap-Martin peninsula. Up above are the winding streets, vaulted passageways and 10th-century château of the original village (see p104).

4 Séguret
Encircling its hillside like a belt, Séguret stares out from the edges of the Dentelles de Montmirail mountains across the nearby wine plain. It's an almost impossibly pretty spot of tiny, pedestrianized streets, medieval edifices and contemporary artists and artisans (see p129).

9 Cassis
Cassis is overseen by France's highest coastal cliffs, whose scale reinforces the intimacy of the narrow little harbour and old town centre down below. Tourists crowd the beaches – the best bathing is in the creeks to the west – but Cassis remains a fishing port, and retains its authenticity (see p82).

5 St-Paul-de-Vence
St-Paul-de-Vence was a farming community living quietly within its medieval surroundings and 16th-century walls until the 1920s. Then it was discovered by the Côte d'Azur artistic community (Picasso, Matisse, Léger) and has been fashionable ever since, with good reason. Both artists and tourists find the tiny streets, ramparts and church remains utterly charming (see p116).

6 Bormes-les-Mimosas
This delightful village seems to tumble down the hillside, with a jumble of steep alleyways, hidden corners and stone houses overcome with flowers – the village's name is very appropriate. Walk up to the top of the hill and enjoy the splendid views of the Mediterranean from the ruined medieval castle (see p89).

The fishing port at Cassis

10 Fontaine-de-Vaucluse
The *"fontaine"* is actually Europe's most powerful natural spring – it pumps out 2.5 million cubic m (55 million gallons) of water a day, and is the source of the River Sorgue. It's a spectacular setting for a lovely village, made even more romantic by its association with the Italian poet, Petrarch, who lived here in the 14th century (see p126).

7 Roussillon
Roussillon is perched magnificently above an extraordinary landscape. The mining of ochre and subsequent erosion have sculpted

TOP10 Areas of Natural Beauty

Lac d'Allos, Parc National du Mercantour

1 Parc National du Mercantour

MAP G2

Mercantour National Park, sprawling over 700 sq km (270 sq miles), is one of Europe's largest, and its rocky slopes are home to rare species including chamois, ibex, moufflon and marmot. Golden eagles and the rare lammergeier vulture soar above the peaks (see p114).

2 Gorges du Cians and Gorges du Dalius

High in the mountains of Haute-Provence and the Alpes-Maritimes, the parallel canyons of the Gorges du Cians and the Gorges du Dalius are awesome ravines, carved by icy fast-flowing streams running down from wine-red cliffs. The main landmark is the Gardienne des Gorges, a huge boulder shaped like a woman's head, standing at the north end of the Gorges du Dalius (see p113).

3 Parc Naturel Régional du Luberon

The Luberon region contains a wide range of habitats. The northern mountains are wild and exposed, while the central massif shelters the southern slopes, creating a gentler environment. Moorland, cedar forest, chalk hills and deep river gorges shelter wild boar, eagles, owls and beavers (see p125).

4 Parc National de Port-Cros

MAP F6

Port-Cros is the smallest of the Îles d'Hyères, and the national park protects the delightful island and 18 sq km (7 sq miles) of sea around it from the development that has overtaken so much of the coast. On land, it shelters beautiful butterflies and rare sea birds, while the clear waters offer excellent scuba diving and snorkelling (see p91).

5 Mont Ventoux

The dramatic peak of Mont Ventoux, at 1,910 m (6,260 ft), seems to guard the gateway to the region. Bare of trees, its higher slopes are known as the *désert de pierre* (stone desert) and are snow-covered from December to April. It has featured in the Tour de France, and even the strongest cyclists dread the treacherous ascent (see p125).

The peak of Mont Ventoux

6 Les Alpilles
MAP B4

The chalky hills of the "Little Alps" rise no higher than 500 m (1,640 ft) but display an arid beauty. This miniature sierra stretches for 24 km (15 miles) between the rivers Rhône and Durance, and the GR6 hiking trail which crosses it is one of the finest walks in Provence.

7 The Camargue

A landscape of lagoons, marshes, wild bulls and France's only cowboys (see pp26–7).

8 Gorges du Loup

The clifftop village of Gourdon, set in rugged limestone country, stands above the dramatic Gorges du Loup, the most accessible of the gorges and canyons that slash through this craggy landscape. The Loup stream plunges over high cascades and has carved deep pot-holes such as the Saut du Loup ("Wolf's Leap") (see p115).

9 Massif des Maures

Thickly wooded with forests of cork and holm oak, pine, myrtle and sweet chestnut, the dramatic Massif des Maures is wild, hilly and sparsely inhabited, even though it is only a stone's throw from the busy coastal hotspots. It is home to France's only surviving wild tortoises, and makes a welcome change from crowded beaches (see p89).

10 Réserve Géologique de Haute-Provence
MAP E2

If dinosaurs and fossils are your thing, this park in the limestone country around Digne is the place to head for. It is the largest of its kind in Europe, covering 1,900 sq km (730 sq miles) of rock, rich in fossils from ancient seas and tropical forests dating back 300 million years.

Waterfall in the Gorges du Loup

🔟 Gardens of Provence

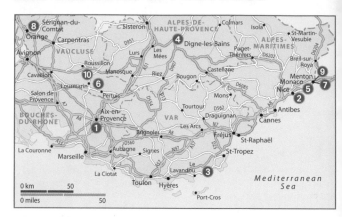

1 Jardins d'Albertas, Bouc-Bel-Air

MAP D4 ▪ DN 8 ▪ 04 42 22 94 71
▪ Open May, Sep, Oct: 2–6pm
weekends and pub hols; Jun–Aug:
3–7pm daily ▪ Adm ▪ www.
jardinsalbertas.com

Laid out in the 1750s, these terraced gardens remain a majestic mix of French and Italian influences – ordered in the geometrical style of France, but with the fountains and statuary favoured by Italy.

Jardin de la Villa Ephrussi de Rothschild

2 Jardin de la Villa Ephrussi de Rothschild, St-Jean-Cap-Ferrat

Baroness Rothschild's mansion is legendary (see p103), and its gardens are of similar sumptuousness. Seven themed areas (Spanish, Florentine, Japanese and more) are rich with plants, sculptures and fountains, and the views are exquisite.

3 Domaine du Rayol, Le Rayol-Canadel

MAP F5 ▪ Av des Belges ▪ Open from 9:30am daily; for closing times visit www.domainedurayol.org ▪ DA
▪ Adm (includes guided tour)

On one of the most magnificent sites on the coast, Rayol offers an overview of Mediterranean-style plant life. Gathered around a pergola and long stairway, a fine mosaic of eight gardens recreates landscapes of areas of the world with Mediterranean climates.

4 Jardin Botanique des Cordeliers, Digne-les-Bains

MAP E2 ▪ Av Paul Martin ▪ Open mid-Mar–mid-Nov: 9am–noon, 2–6pm Tue–Fri (to 7pm Jul–Aug) ▪ Closed Mon am ▪ Guided tours in English by appt: 04 92 31 59 59 ▪ DA

Named after a 13th-century convent previously on the site, this garden features more than 650 species of aromatic plants from the region and abroad. Beds are arranged in squares, according to a classical design.

Cacti in the Jardin Exotique

5 Jardin Exotique, Monaco

Crisscrossed by winding paths, this garden features a large collection of cactuses, succulents and other semi-desert plants – 6,000 varieties in all. A prehistoric cave and anthropology museum are also within the garden grounds *(see p107)*.

6 Château Val Joanis, Pertuis

MAP D4 ■ D973 ■ 04 90 79 20 77 ■ Open 10am–7pm daily (winter: 10am–1pm & 2–5:30pm Mon–Sat) ■ Adm

These award-winning gardens were planted in 1978 on three sheltered terraces, mimicking the 17th-century French style. They include a classic *potager* (vegetable garden) and an orchard amid roses and cypresses.

7 Serre de la Madone, Menton

MAP H3 ■ 74 rte de Gorbio ■ 04 93 57 73 90 ■ Open 10am–6pm Tue–Sun (to 5pm Jan–Mar); guided tours 3pm daily ■ Closed Nov, Dec ■ Adm ■ www.serredelamadone.com

Anglo-American Lawrence Johnston was a leader among expats who left their mark on Riviera gardens in the early 20th century. His hillside spread is so well landscaped, it barely seems structured. Terraces harbour enclosed spaces dedicated to themes or particular exotic plants, and there are fountains, water gardens and a collection of statues.

8 Harmas Jean-Henri Fabré, Sérignan-du-Comtat

MAP B2 ■ Rte d'Orange ■ 04 90 30 57 62 ■ Opening times vary by season; visit www.harmasjeanhenrifabre.fr for details ■ Adm

This fascinating walled garden was planted by etymologist Jean-Henri Fabre to observe the lives of insects, which he recorded in exquisite watercolours in his books.

9 Jardin Botanique Exotique du Val Rahmeh, Menton

MAP H3 ■ Av St Jacques ■ Open 10am–12:30pm, 2–5pm Wed–Mon (Apr–Sep: 10am–12:30pm, 3:30–6:30pm) ■ Closed 1 May, 25 Dec ■ Adm

More than 700 tropical plants crowd these terraces, established in 1905 by Lord Radcliff, a former governor of Malta. Val Rahmeh specializes in spices, wildflowers, medicinal plants, succulents and rare varieties of tomato and potato.

10 Jardin de la Louve, Bonnieux

MAP C3 ■ Chemin St Gervais ■ Open for tours only (email: pascalverger@me.com to book an appt) ■ www.lalouve.eu ■ Adm

It's worth the special effort to visit this private, ultra-contemporary topiary garden, created by Hermès stylist Nicole de Vésian to harmonize with the surrounding landscape.

Water garden in Serre de la Madone

🔟 Beaches in Provence

Dramatic Calanque d'En-Vau

port to the loveliest beach in France (see p91). Pine-fringed, it boasts white sand, clear, calm waters, no commerce and few people – your private slice of paradise.

① Calanque d'En-Vau, Cassis

Calanques are inlets formed where the chalk cliffs plunge to the sea; many are found between Cassis and Marseille. En-Vau is the prettiest and one of the more accessible – a 90-minute walk from the nearest Cassis car park. At the foot of the white, pine-clad rocks, the setting of sand and luminous sea is intimate, wild and unforgettable (see pp76–7).

② Plage de Notre Dame, Île de Porquerolles
MAP E6

No cars are allowed on the island, so it's a walk or cycle-ride along the rocky, 3-km (2-mile) track from the

③ Plage de Pampelonne, St-Tropez
MAP F5

Everyone has his or her "place" on St-Trop's largest beach. Famous beach clubs cater to the super-rich and glamorous, to nudists, to gay people, as well as to everyday families. The 5-km (3-mile) sandy stretch across the headland from the town also has extensive public areas. There's space in which to escape the crowds and appreciate natural beauty (see p25).

④ Plage de la Garoupe, Cap d'Antibes

Between them, Antibes and Juan-les-Pins have 25 km (16 miles) of coast and 48 beaches, slotted into rocky creeks or opening out into sandy expanses. The prettiest is la Garoupe, on an inlet of the peninsula. It's highly fashionable and very crowded in summer – but with very good reason (see p110).

⑤ Plage d'Agay, St-Raphaël

As the red rocks of the Esterel hills tumble into the clear blue sea, they give the coastline around St-Raphaël an untamed allure. The small creeks are enticing; equally

Esterel coastline around Plage d'Agay

alluring, but bigger, sandier and more accessible, is the Bay of Agay – perfect for families (see p106).

6 Plage de l'Eléphant, Le Lavandou
MAP F5

Le Lavandou has 12 beaches covering the full seaside spectrum, from the great sandy stretch of the Grande Plage to the nudist creek of Rossignol. L'Eléphant is the most appealing. The approach is only by sea or over rocks, a feature which usually ensures relative tranquillity.

Sunbathers enjoy Plage de l'Eléphant

7 St-Honorat, Îles de Lérins

A short ferry ride leads from the crowds of Cannes to this island owned by Cistercian monks (see p57). The presence of the monastery seems to discourage the more brazen holiday-makers so the pretty rock outcrops and tiny beaches here remain calm and, unusually for Provence, positively underpopulated.

Calanque de Figuerolles

8 Calanque de Figuerolles, La Ciotat
MAP D5

Steps on the eastern edge of town lead to this extraordinary creek. On either side are cliffs, while further back are terraces of fig trees and pines. Out front, the blue sea laps around weird rock formations. It is a world unto itself.

9 Plage de St-Aygulf, Fréjus
MAP F5

Long, wide, sandy and safe, the main beach at St-Aygulf, near Fréjus (see p87), has the additional advantage of being in a Nature Preservation Area. This protects the Étangs de Villepey – great, wild, freshwater lagoons on the other side of the road, where 217 different bird species have been noted.

10 Piémançon Beach, The Camargue
MAP B5

This is a beach beyond civilization. You must thread your way between salt flats and lagoons before arriving at the flat, exposed sands of France's last truly "wild beach".

🔟 Offshore Islands

View from Port-Cros, one of the Îles d'Hyères

1 Port-Cros, Îles d'Hyères

A national park (see p50), the smallest and most mountainous of the Hyères isles is dense with pine woods and oaks. Paths lead up to clifftops offering dramatic views. For relaxation, La Palud is by far the best beach.

2 Le Levant, Îles d'Hyères
MAP F6 ▪ Ferry from Hyères

Although 90 per cent of this island is a French Navy missile base, the other 10 per cent is a naturist colony. Clothes must be worn in the village but not beyond.

3 Îles du Frioul
MAP C5 ▪ Ferry from Vieux Port, Marseille

The linked islands of Ratonneau and Pomègues guard Marseille harbour (see p75). Beyond Port Frioul, white rocks ruggedly conceal unspoiled little beaches. The diving and snorkelling here is renowned.

4 Île d'If
MAP C5 ▪ Ferry from Vieux Port, Marseille

This prison island is most famous as the place from which Dumas' fictional Count of Monte Cristo escaped (see p41). You may even visit the "Count's dungeon".

5 Ste-Marguérite, Îles de Lérins
MAP G4 ▪ Ferry from Cannes harbour

Ste-Marguérite offers woods of pine and eucalyptus and stony coves. In 1687, the Man in the Iron Mask was imprisoned in the fort here (see p38).

6 Porquerolles, Îles d'Hyères
MAP E6 ▪ Ferry from La Tour-Fondue, near Giens

The largest of the French Riviera islands is the car-free hideaway of Porquerolles. Hire a bike or explore on foot to appreciate this paradise of vineyards, olive groves, scented forests and glorious beaches.

Tranquil beach in Porquerolles

7 **Îles des Embiez**
MAP D6 ■ Ferry from Le Brusc, near Six-Fours-les-Plages ■ www.les-embiez.com

The larger of two islands developed for tourism by drinks magnate Paul Ricard, Embiez is a delight. Development has been sensitively merged into the landscape, leaving most of the island's creeks, woods and salt marshes untouched.

8 **St-Honorat, Îles de Lérins**
MAP G4 ■ 04 92 99 54 00 ■ Ferry from Cannes ■ Fortified monastery: Open Jul–mid-Sep: 10am–noon, 2:30–5pm daily (rest of monastery closed); mid-Sep–Jun: 7am–6pm daily ■ www.abbayedelerins.com

St-Honorat has been run by monks almost continually since the 5th century. The 11th-century fortified monastery is a must-see. The monks make their own wine here, which can be bought in the shop.

St-Honorat's fortified monastery

9 **Bendor**
MAP D5 ■ Ferry from Bandol

Embiez's baby brother has a tiny harbour and beaches – you can do the tour in 20 minutes. But the tourist development is as sensitive as on Embiez, and complements the natural landscape beautifully.

10 **Île Verte**
MAP D5 ■ Ferry from Vieux Port, La Ciotat

The "Verte" of its name refers to the island's greenery, notably the trees topping the steep cliffs. Billed as "one of the last virgin islands of the Mediterranean coast", the islet has tiny creeks and beaches.

TOP 10 ISLAND ACTIVITIES

Cycling on Porquerolles

1 Cycling
On Porquerolles and Embiez, cycle the forest paths to creeks and beaches.

2 Snorkelling, Port-Cros
National Park Office ■ 04 94 01 40 70 ■ www.portcrosparcnational.fr
Follow a signposted underwater "nature trail" from La Palud.

3 Fort Ste-Agathe, Porquerolles
Open mid-Jun–mid-Sep for guided tours 10am, 2pm, 4pm ■ 04 94 58 07 24 ■ Adm ■ www.porquerolles.com
Exhibitions on the region's nature.

4 Diving, Embiez
Centre de Plongée ■ 06 87 61 03 20
Courses in water rich with marine life.

5 Lighthouse Walk, Porquerolles
A 90-minute round trip to one of the finest lighthouses.

6 Fort de l'Estissac, Port-Cros
Open May–Oct, 10:30am–12.30pm, 2–5pm
Exhibits on local history.

7 Aquascope, Embiez
Open Apr–Oct ■ 04 94 34 17 85 ■ Adm
A glass "bubble" over water allows close encounters of a marine kind.

8 Sailing and Sea Kayaking, Bendor
Société Nautique de Bendor ■ bendor.com
Hire and classes in summer.

9 Vallon de la Solitude Walk, Port-Cros
A two-hour walk through shady forest to the Fort de la Vigie.

10 Universal Wine and Spirits Exhibition, Bendor
Open Jul–Aug: 1–6pm Thu–Tue ■ 04 94 05 15 61 ■ www.euvs.org
A display of 8,000 bottles from over 50 countries.

TOP 10 Places to See and Be Seen

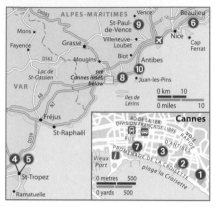

Cannes' exorbitantly luxurious seafront hotels, overlooks the Croisette and is the top place to see and be seen in town, with a magnificent view of the bay (see p110).

③ Le Petit Majestic, Cannes

MAP G4 ■ 6 rue Tony Allard ■ 04 93 39 94 92

This night hangout is popular with the late crowd, who party until the early hours all summer long. During the film festival you'll find the cream of the world's movie business here (see p70).

① La Palme d'Or, Cannes

MAP G4 ■ 73 bd de la Croisette ■ 04 92 98 74 14 ■ DA ■ €€€

The restaurant at the Hotel Martinez is where stars dine, as the signed photos in the foyer attest, and the menu is suitably opulent. Dress to kill and prepare to reach your credit card limit.

② Carlton InterContinental, Cannes

The spacious terrace in front of the Carlton InterContinental, one of

Carlton InterContinental, Cannes

④ Les Caves du Roy, St-Tropez

To mingle with the rich and famous, book a room at St-Trop's most stylish hotel and swan into Les Caves du Roy, the hotel's nightclub. In season it's the haunt of supermodels, film stars and racing drivers. Wear your most fabulous outfit (see p92).

⑤ Club 55, Ramatuelle, St-Tropez

MAP F5 ■ Plage de Pampelonne, bd Patch ■ 04 94 55 55 55 ■ DA ■ €€€

Ever since Le Cinquante Cinq first opened in 1955, its guest list has been like reading an A to Z of the rich and famous. Book ahead if you want a table in the restaurant, dress to impress and bring your platinum credit card. Open summer only.

⑥ Zelo, Beaulieu Port

MAP H4 ■ Port de Plaisance, Promenade Pasteur ■ 04 93 01 11 00 ■ DA

Don your best bikini and sashay down to one of the Riviera's hippest beaches, Zélo, which attracts a star-studded crowd. Sunbeds start at €25 for half a day; there's a restaurant, Wi-Fi and late-night partying.

Sun and dining terrace of the Hotel Le Majestic Barrière, Cannes

⑦ Hotel Le Majestic Barrière, Cannes

One of the flashiest café-terraces in town attracts a high-spending, fashionable clientele year-round, and some of the world's brightest stars during the film festival – Robert De Niro, Matthew McConaughey and Jake Gyllenhaal have been sighted. Anything stronger than coffee costs a fortune (see p110).

⑧ Tetou, Golfe Juan

MAP G4 ▪ 8 av des Frères Roustan ▪ 04 93 63 71 16 ▪ Closed Nov–Mar, Wed, and Mon–Tue lunch ▪ No credit cards ▪ €€€

Superb *bouillabaisse* has been the raison d'être of Tetou since it opened right on Golfe Juan's beach in 1920. During the Cannes Film Festival, it's booked out with Hollywood stars and its chic beach is one of the biggest on the coast.

⑨ Le St-Paul, St-Paul-de-Vence

Nestled away in the heart of the medieval village, celebrities love Le St Paul's exclusive atmosphere, elegant dining room and walled garden terrace, with tables and comfy wicker chairs surrounding a 17th-century fountain. The cuisine,

by young Provençale chef Richard Vicens, is creative Mediterranean (try the slow-cooked sea bass). At night, the restaurant is pure romance, illuminated by hundreds of flickering candles (see p117).

⑩ Hotel du Cap-Eden-Roc, Cap d'Antibes

Book years ahead to mingle with the rich and famous at this luxurious hotel. The model for the hotel in F Scott Fitzgerald's *Tender is the Night*, it was the flagship of Riviera hedonism. The list of celebrity guests stretches back decades and includes such stars as Johnny Depp, Gwyneth Paltrow and Leonardo DiCaprio (see p143).

Suite at the Hotel du Cap-Eden-Roc

For a key to restaurant price ranges see p79

🔟 Vineyards and Distilleries

Châtau Romanin's vaulted cellar

The Cuvée Clos d'Ière is among the most expressive of Provençal wines. The welcome at the cellar is both easy and relaxed. There is also a hotel and a restaurant.

① Château Romanin
MAP B3 ■ Mas Romanin, St-Rémy-de-Provence ■ 04 90 92 45 87

This stunning underground winery resembles a cathedral, and the site has had spiritual associations since the Greeks worshipped here in the 4th century BC. The owners' methods reflect this past, including cultivation by the phases of the moon.

② Château Ste-Roseline
MAP F4 ■ Sauteraine, Les-Arcs-sur-Argens ■ 04 94 99 50 30

The château's Côtes-de-Provence wines have improved greatly in recent times. Its Cuvée Prieuré can age for 15 years or more, making it more than worthy of its historic surroundings. The château and grounds also host summer concerts.

③ Domaine Rabiéga
MAP F4 ■ Clos d'Ière, 516 Chemin Cros d'Aimar, Draguignan ■ 04 94 68 44 22

Set within a wooded residential suburb, this French-run domain has an innovative attitude to wine quality.

④ Distilleries & Domaines de Provence
MAP D3 ■ 9 av St-Promasse, Forcalquier ■ www.distilleries-provence.com

Home of Henri Bardouin, the connoisseur's *pastis*. Like all *pastis*, Bardouin is based on star anise, but here they add 50 other herbs and spices, many of them local. The result is an apéritif more richly flavoured than other brands.

⑤ Domaine de Beaurenard
MAP B3 ■ 10 av Pierre de Luxembourg, Châteauneuf-du-Pape ■ 04 90 83 71 79

The Coulon family have been here in Provence's most famous wine village since 1695 – time enough to really perfect their skills. The Boisrenard red is the proof. They also run the region's best wine museum.

⑥ Château de Berne
MAP F4 ■ Rte de Salernes, Lorgues ■ 04 94 60 43 52

British-owned Berne is the region's best wine visitors' centre. The site is picturesque, the welcome friendly, and there's a full calendar of cultural events. There's also a first-class hotel-restaurant on site, L'Auberge. The best wine is the Cuvée Spéciale.

Pretty surrounds of Château de Berne

⑦ Château La Coste
MAP C4 ■ Rte de la Cride, Le-Puy-Ste-Réparade ■ 04 42 61 92 90

Irish businessman Patrick McKillen's biodynamic vineyard features a contemporary art promenade with works by Louise Bourgeois and Tracey Emin, among others, and striking buildings by Jean Nouvel, Frank Gehry and Tadao Ando.

⑧ Domaine de la Citadelle
MAP C3 ■ Rte de Cavaillon, Ménerbes ■ 04 90 72 41 58

Former film producer and politician Yves Rousset-Rouard sunk a fortune into this stylish set-up. The Côtes-de-Luberon wines are treated with respect, and the on-site Corkscrew Museum is unique.

Domaine de la Citadelle

⑨ Domaine St André de Figuière
MAP E5 ■ BP47, Quartier St Honoré, La Londe-les-Maures ■ 04 94 00 44 70

In a superb location, set back from the sea and next to a bird sanctuary, Alain Combard and his family make wines of great finesse. Note that the visitors' entrance to the cellar is round the back of a steel tank.

⑩ Château de Pibarnon
MAP D5 ■ Comte de St Victor, La Cadière-d'Azur ■ 04 94 90 12 73

Perched directly above the sea, this may be the most attractively sited wine château in Provence. Owner Henri de Saint-Victor has wrestled the unyielding land to produce delicious red wines now in the forefront of the Bandol appellation.

TOP 10 REGIONAL WINES

Vineyards in Bandol

1 Châteauneuf-du-Pape
At their best, the reds are dark and powerful, while the (rarer) whites are intensely fruity.

2 Bandol
The home of the Mourvèdre grape produces fine and vigorous reds.

3 Beaumes de Venise
France's richest fortified dessert wine, made from the Muscat grape.

4 Côtes-de-Provence
Famed for rosés, this region is now also producing classy reds and heady whites.

5 Gigondas
Sometimes known as "son of Châteauneuf-du-Pape" but the full-bodied wines definitely stand out on their own.

6 Côteaux d'Aix-en-Provence
Fast-improving red and rosé wines.

7 Cassis
Fresh, dry whites – particularly good served with Provençal fish dishes.

8 Côtes du Ventoux
The reds, especially, can be very rewarding – although rosés are great for summer picnics.

9 Côtes du Luberon
Another hugely improved group of wines, not least due to investment from fashionable outsiders.

10 Côtes-du-Rhône Villages
In theory, one step up from ordinary Côtes-du-Rhône, but they can be several steps up in practice – especially if the name of the village (such as Cairanne) is mentioned on the label.

🔟 Children's Activities

Tropical fish at Marineland

1 Marineland, Antibes
MAP G4 ▪ 5Rte National 7, Antibes ▪ Open hours vary by season ▪ DA ▪ Adm ▪ www.marineland.fr

Provence's biggest aquatic theme park has a full range of activities especially designed for younger children, including a petting zoo, miniature golf and a pool.

2 Kayaking, Fontaine-de-Vaucluse
MAP C3 ▪ Fontaine-de-Vaucluse ▪ 04 90 20 35 44 ▪ Open mid-Apr–mid-Oct ▪ No credit cards

After gushing from its source at Fontaine de Vaucluse (see p126) the river Sorgue becomes idyllic, perfect for a lazy two-hour paddle downstream. Kayak Vert Aqueduc canoes hold two adults and two children; life jackets and return shuttle included.

3 Musée Oceanographic, Monaco
As well as its superb aquariums, with over 6,000 species of marine life, the Oceanographic Museum has a terrace overlooking the sea and an enclosure for African spurred turtles. During the school holidays, book a special ticket for the Touch Tank, where children can pet starfish and a baby shark (see p104).

4 Azur Park, St-Tropez
MAP F5 ▪ 51 Rond-Point de la Foux, Gassin ▪ Open Apr–Sep ▪ Adm ▪ azurpark.fr/en

Located just outside St-Tropez, this funfair is a local institution. There are 35 attractions to choose from, including rides for toddlers. Children also adore the prehistoric mini-golf course, featuring model dinosaurs and woolly mammoths.

Aerial view of Aqualand, Fréjus

5 Aqualand, Fréjus
MAP F5 ▪ 462 RD 559 ▪ Open mid-Jun–mid-Sep: 10am–6pm (mid Jul–Aug: to 7pm) ▪ Adm

One of the biggest water parks in Provence, this offers fun for all ages, from daredevil slides and white water thrills to calmer pools and toddler activities in the Children's Paradise.

⑥ Château de la Barben, La Barben

MAP C4 ■ Route du Château ■ Open Feb school hols, Mar, mid-Sep–mid-Oct: 2–5pm Sat–Sun; Apr–mid-Sep: 11am–6pm; mid-Oct–early Nov: 2–5pm ■ Adm ■ www.chateaudelabarben.fr

In this striking medieval castle high on a hill, knights greet visitors in the dungeon and describe life in the 13th century over the course of a tour. There's a riddle game for children to solve while exploring the castle, with a prize at the end, and treasure hunts in the château grounds.

Trebuchets at Les-Baux-de-Provence

⑦ Crossbows and Catapults, Les-Baux-de-Provence

Life-sized siege engines – a ballista, catapults, trebuchets and a battering ram – bring medieval warfare to life at the dramatic fortified castle of Les Baux. Special children's activities (including training in shooting crossbows) take place during medieval festivals during the holidays and on summer weekends *(see p82).*

⑧ Les Marais du Vigueirat, Camargue

MAP B4 ■ Chemin de l'Etourneau, Arles ■ Open 9:30am–5pm daily (to 5:30pm Apr–Sep) ■ Closed Dec–mid-Jan ■ Adm

A great place for families to explore the Camargue, Vigueirat has signposted paths and nature tours for ages six and up, with the chance to see herds of white horses, black bulls, pink flamingoes, wild boar and more on horse-drawn carriage rides.

⑨ Le Villages des Automates, St-Cannat

MAP C4 ■ Chemin de la Dilligence ■ Open Apr–mid-Sep: 10am–6pm daily (Jul & Aug: to 7pm); mid-Sep–Mar: 10am–5pm Wed, Sat, Sun, public hols and school hols ■ Adm

Animated automata bring storybooks to life in a series of themed tableaux, set in a wooded park. Characters include Scheherazade, Gulliver in Lilliput and Pinocchio and the whale. There's also a petting zoo, adventure park with ziplines, an elevated miniature railway, a tricycle race course and a massive indoor playpark.

⑩ La Ferme aux Crocodiles, Pierrelatte

MAP B2 ■ 395 allée de Beauplan ■ Open daily; Mar–Jun, Sep–Oct: 10am–6pm; Jul–Aug: 9:30am–7pm; Nov–Feb: 10am–5pm ■ Adm

Ten species of crocodile in a large indoor lagoon are the stars of the show, but the farm also has snakes and other reptiles (including giant Seychelles tortoises), fish and exotic birds in a tropical garden setting. On weekends at 11:30am, visitors can watch the feeding of the reptiles.

La Ferme aux Crocodiles

☰☷ **Sporting Activities**

Skier in the Alpes-Maritimes

1 Skiing

Skiing is concentrated where Provence and the Alps meet *(see p114)*. In the Ubaye valley, Pra-Loup, Le Sauze and Super-Sauze offer international-standard facilities as, in the Allos valley, do La Foux and Seignus. Meanwhile, there's family-friendly skiing on Mont Ventoux – notably at Mont Serein.

2 Climbing

For some of France's finest, toughest rock climbing, head for the Buoux cliffs in the Luberon *(see p125)*, the Gorges du Verdon, with their 933 routes *(see pp14–15)* or the creeks and Calanques between Marseille and Cassis *(see pp76–7)*. Easier conditions can be found in the Dentelles de Montmirail *(see p126)*.

Climbing in the Gorges du Verdon

3 Sailing

Almost all the coastal resorts have well-equipped pleasure ports and cater for both the beginner and the experienced. The islands of Porquerolles and Bendor *(see pp56–7)* have renowned sailing schools.

4 Canoeing

The classic river trip is to canoe down the Gorges du Verdon – a two-day, turbulent, 24-km (15-mile) trip from Carrejuan Bridge to Lac de Ste-Croix *(see p15)*. Less adventurous canoeists might prefer paddling the gentler Sorgue, from Fontaine-de-Vaucluse *(see p126)*.

Canoeing on the Verdon river

5 Mountain Biking

The marked trails, up and down mountains, through vineyards, forests, gorges and creeks, are endlessly inviting. Figanières is a key centre in the Upper Var, while the Alpes-de-Haute-Provence region has some 1,500 km (900 miles) of marked tracks.

6 Golf

The finest golfing can be found at the Frégate golf course, St Cyr, where the sea views are sensational *(see p91)*. Other courses offering good golf in lovely surroundings include the Golf de l'Esterel at St-Raphaël, the Ballesteros-designed Pont-Royal at Mallemort and Golf de Châteaublanc outside Avignon.

7 Scuba Diving

The richness of marine life, clear waters and a sprinkling of wrecks all draw divers to the Mediterannean coast. The Îles d'Hyères are noted for their seascapes and for the underwater "discovery trail" on Port-Cros (see p56). Cavalaire and Marseille remain, however, the best-equipped centres.

8 Canyoning

The exhilarating sport of descending torrents and canyons by abseiling, jumping and swimming has taken off big time. Try it in the Roya valley near Saorge or in any of 70 sites in the Ubaye and Verdon valleys. There are some easier descents for beginners in the Pennafort and Destel gorges.

9 Walking

From the coastal paths to mountain tracks inland, Provence could have been created for walkers. Strollers may amble around bays or along woodland paths, while serious hikers can take to the National Hiking Trails (Grandes Randonnées or GR) which crisscross the region.

10 Windsurfing

The breezy Var and Bouches-du-Rhône coasts are ideal for water-sports fans. As the Mistral whistles across the Camargue, so windsurfers take advantage at Saintes-Maries-de-la-Mer and Port-St-Louis (see p26).

Windsurfing on the Var

TOP 10 WALKS

Hiking in the Mercantour

1 Vallée des Merveilles, Mercantour National Park
Only serious hikers should attempt this marvellous mountain trek. Allow 2–3 days, overnighting in refuges. Contact Park HQ before setting out (see p114).

2 Martel Trail, Verdon Gorges
A breathtaking 15 km (9 mile) trail from Le Palud to Point Sublime. Allow 7–8 hours (see p14).

3 Calanques, Marseille
Spectacular walking along rugged headland trails (see p76).

4 Massif des Maures
The forests, valleys and peaks are covered with excellent trails (see p91).

5 Coastal Path, Six-Fours-les-Plages
MAP D6
The seaside walk to La Seyne starts off flat, then climbs to the Cap Sicié for fantastic views. Allow 7 hours.

6 Baou de St-Jeannet, St-Jeannet
MAP G4
This stiff but rewarding walk (3–4 hours) ascends the "baou" – the rock overlooking the village near Vence.

7 Port-Cros, Îles d'Hyères
Take in a paradise of forests, creeks and headlands as you walk the coast in 5 hours (see p56).

8 Dentelles de Montmirail
Trek from Sablet up to St Amand, the highest point. Six hours (see p126).

9 Vieux Nice
From the Old Town up to Castle Hill and down again: the best in-town walking in the region (see pp20–21).

10 Massif de l'Esterel
The very best mountain path is from Pont de l'Esterel to Mont Vinaigre. Allow 4 hours (see p88).

🔟 Gourmet Restaurants

Louis XV restaurant at the Hôtel de Paris, Monte Carlo

1 Louis XV, Monte Carlo
MAP H4 ▪ Hôtel de Paris, pl du Casino ▪ 003 77 98 06 88 64 ▪ Closed L, Tue, Wed (except mid-Jun–Sep), late Feb–mid-Mar, Dec ▪ DA ▪ €€€

The world's most glamorous diners expect splendour, and will get it here amid wood panelling, gilded mirrors and chandeliers. A team of top chefs takes centre stage to cook Alain Ducasse's exquisite interpretations of Provençal cuisine.

2 Atelier Rabanel, Arles
MAP B4 ▪ 7 rue des Carmes ▪ 04 90 91 07 69 ▪ Closed Mon–Tue, last week in Feb ▪ DA ▪ €€€

Jean-Luc Rabanel is the first organic chef to receive a Michelin star. The menu depends on what vegetables have been picked from the kitchen garden, and on Chef's imagination.

Plating up at Atelier Rabanel, Arles

3 Le Chantecler, Nice
Within the palatial Negresco hotel (see p143), Le Chantecler boasts Regency decor and wood panelling. The service is exquisite, as is chef Jean-Denis Rieubland's imaginative food (see p99).

4 La Bastide de Capelongue, Bonnieux
Young chef Edouard Loubet has a huge reputation for Provençal cooking of great finesse. The surroundings are equally fine (see p131).

5 La Vague d'Or, St-Tropez
MAP F5 ▪ Résidence de la Pinede, plage de la Bouillabaisse ▪ 04 94 55 91 00 ▪ Closed L, mid-Oct–mid-Apr ▪ DA ▪ €€€

At the chic beachside Résidence de la Pinede (see p142), chef Arnaud Donckele prepares unforgettable dishes in a dreamy setting.

6 L'Oasis, La Napoule
MAP G4 ▪ Rue Jean-Honoré-Carle ▪ 04 93 49 95 52 ▪ Closed mid-Nov–mid-Jan, Mon, Sun (Oct–Apr) ▪ €€€ (bistro €€)

In a Neo-Gothic villa overlooking La Napoule port, culinary magic is performed by the three Raimbault brothers. The rooftop bistro offers menus at more affordable prices.

(7) Le Petit Nice Passédat, Marseille

Anse de Maldormé, Corniche J F Kennedy ■ 04 91 59 25 92 ■ Closed Sun–Mon, 1–20 Jan, Feb school hols & Nov ■ DA ■ €€€

Perched on a cliff overlooking the sea, this luxury hotel houses Marseille's first three-star Michelin restaurant. Try beignets of sea anemones or the line-caught sea bass, followed by a delicious dark chocolate and raspberry delight.

(8) Chevre d'Or, Èze

MAP H4 ■ 6 rue du Barri ■ 04 92 10 66 66 ■ Closed early Nov–early Mar, L Mon–Wed (except Jul & Aug) ■ €€€

A Riviera legend, the "Golden Goat" combines stupendous views over the coast with exquisite, beautifully presented seasonal dishes.

L'Oustau de Baumanière

(9) L'Oustau de Baumanière, Les-Baux-de-Provence

MAP B4 ■ CD 27 ■ 04 90 54 33 07 ■ Closed Dec–Feb ■ €€€

This converted farmstead dates from the 14th century; the two-Michelin-starred food marries fresh, seasonal local produce with top-class cuisine.

(10) Bastide St-Antoine, Grasse

This restored 18th-century country house is superbly set amid lavender and olive trees above Grasse. Equally splendid is the cooking by chef Jacques Chibois (see p117).

TOP 10 REGIONAL SPECIALITIES

Provençal *bouillabaisse*

1 Bouillabaisse
Marseille fish dish of up to three species. The spicy cooking juices are served as a soup before the fish itself.

2 Salade Niçoise
Purists use only raw vegetables, hard-boiled eggs, anchovies, olives and olive oil, but tuna is usually added, too.

3 Olives
A signature Provençal product, olives were introduced by the Greeks in the 4th century BC, and olive oil is central to regional dishes.

4 Aïoli
Garlic mayonnaise made with olive oil. Accompanies raw vegetables, cold cod and hard-boiled eggs.

5 Pistou
Thick soup of haricot and kidney beans, pasta and other vegetables, with basil, garlic and olive oil.

6 Pieds et paquets
Lamb's feet (*pieds*) and stuffed sheep's stomach (*paquets*) in white wine.

7 Ratatouille
Stew of peppers, courgettes (zucchini), aubergines (eggplant), tomatoes and onions, sautéed in olive oil.

8 Truffles
The season for this highly flavoured, rare underground fungus runs from mid-November to mid-March. Carpentras is the centre (see p127).

9 Daube
Beef (or wild boar) is marinated and slowly simmered in a sauce of red wine with herbs and garlic.

10 Tapenade
Purée of olives, capers, garlic and anchovies. *Anchoïade* is similar, but without capers or olives.

For a key to restaurant price ranges see p79

🔟 Provence for Free

Exhibition at Villa Arson, Nice

1 Contemporary Culture
MAP N1 ■ 20 av Stephen Liégeard, Nice ■ 04 92 07 73 73 ■ Open 2–6pm (Jul & Aug: to 7pm) Wed–Mon (during exhibitions only) ■ www.villa-arson.org

The Villa Arson is a fine art school and contemporary art gallery housed in a bucolic villa in northern Nice. Visitors can enjoy a changing roster of exhibitions focusing on contemporary French sculpture, Parisian Pop Art and video montages.

2 Pedalling Provence
Many hotels offer free bike loan for their guests. The region's larger cities, such as Marseille, Aix and Avignon, also have inexpensive bike share schemes (see p135).

3 Vineyard Tastings
Vines have carpeted Provence and the Côte d'Azur since Roman times. Almost every vineyard offers free tastings to visitors amid bucolic grounds – although buying at least a bottle (at bargain château prices) is considered polite. Even the region's finest vintners (see pp60–61) welcome visitors.

4 Food for Free
MAP B3 ■ pl Pie, Avignon ■ 04 90 27 15 15 ■ www.avignon-leshalles.com/petitecuisine.htm

Every Saturday morning at 11am, one of Avignon's leading chefs cooks up a storm in the city's Les Halles food market. La Petite Cuisine des Halles' programme promises complimentary tastings, recipes and all sorts of culinary tips and techniques.

5 Church Art
For centuries the Catholic church was the most powerful economic force in Provence, and it shows in the masterpieces on its walls: visit, for example, Grasse's Notre-Dame-du-Puy (see p46), where a Fragonard and a trio of Rubens canvases adorn the interior. But you can see works of interest by the Old Masters for free in almost every church and cathedral in the region.

6 Lavender Fields
Blooming lavender fields are best seen from June to early August. Some of the prettiest sights can be seen while driving through Castellet, Gordes, Sault and Forcalquier. The hillside town of Sault draws crowds during its Fête de Lavande, which is held on 15 August.

Lavender fields in bloom, Provence

View of St-Jean-Cap-Ferrat

7 Walk the World's Wealthiest Peninsula

MAP H4

Cap-Ferrat is the world's second-priciest property spot (only Monaco is more expensive). A 6-km (4-mile) public footpath makes its way round the cape, past billionaires' gardens from Plage de Passable beach in Villefranche to David Niven's former home near St-Jean.

8 St-Tropez on a Shoestring

Little comes cheap in Europe's A-list getaway. But while the celebs soak up the sun at exclusive Plage de Pampelonne beach bars such as Club 55 *(see p58)*, the rest of the shore is free to mere mortals. And Le Café on place des Lices *(see p25)* offers guests free use of *pétanque* balls.

9 A Princely View of Monaco

Peer out from the palatial mound of Monte Carlo on a sunny day to glimpse Corsica twinkling in the distance. Whatever the weather, you can see the daily Changing of the Palace Guard *(see p103)*.

10 In the Footsteps of Cézanne

Aix-en-Provence's most famous inhabitant is cemented into history with a walking trail *(see p18)*. Follow the brass floor plaques (with an accompanying leaflet if you wish) that lead you through Cézanne's favourite haunts around town.

TOP 10 MONEY-SAVING TIPS

1 A hotel *petit déjeuner* (breakfast) can cost you upwards of €10. Hit a café for fresh croissants instead, but take note: a *café-crème* or *café au lait* is coffee for tourists. Locals sip a *noisette* instead.

2 Sign up online for one of the region's many city bike share schemes. Nice's Vélib and Marseille's Le Vélo offer bicycles from 50c per hour.

3 Local wine by the *pichet*, or half-litre carafe, will halve your drinks bill. It's also acceptable, when dining, to ask for a *carafe d'eau* (jug of tap water) rather than a bottle of mineral water.

4 Museum passes are a steal. The French Riviera Pass grants free access and discounts to several sites in Nice and along the Côte d'Azur. Students and over-60s often qualify for a discount, and state-owned museums are free to EU students under 26 (ID is required).

5 Book TGV tickets online at *www. voyages-sncf.com* for vast discounts – like Nice to Avignon from €20. Rail passes are great value too.

6 Hotel chains Formule 1 and B&B Hôtel offer bargain, no-frills rooms.

7 City-centre self-catering apartments work out far cheaper than hotels for families staying a few days. The countryside alternatives are *gîtes*.

8 Youth hostels (no age limit) may be found in most major cities and in many national parks. Provençal camp sites are not much cheaper than a budget hotel. Wild camping is discouraged.

9 Provençal markets and shops can supply all you need for the perfect seaside picnic at less than the cost of a café terrace snack.

10 Hitchhiking is permitted on all roads except *autoroutes* (motorways).

Vélib shared bikes in Nice

TOP 10 Festivals and Events

1 Cannes Film Festival
MAP G4 ▪ May

Some 30,000 film professionals attend this world-famous gathering, to do business and, incidentally, see a few films. The atmosphere is glamorously electric. As a member of the public, don't expect to meet, or even see, the stars, except as they mount the steps of the Festival Palace for a screening.

Performer at the Avignon Festival

2 Aix Festival
MAP C4 ▪ Jul

Founded in 1948, this is a great lyrical event. As well as classical opera in the courtyard of the Archbishop's Palace and other venues, there are more contemporary works, recitals by musicians, music masterclasses at its Académie Européenne de Musique and street theatre.

5 Avignon Festival
MAP B3 ▪ Jul

France's greatest theatre event is really two festivals. The official one takes over the Papal Palace's Courtyard of Honour (see p12) and other venues for both modern and classical drama. However, it is the unofficial "off" festival which enlivens the town, with street performers and up to 400 shows a day, from dance to burlesque comedy.

6 International Piano Festival, Roque d'Anthéron
MAP C4 ▪ Mid-Jul–mid-Aug

Since 1980, the festival has drawn the cream of the world's classical and jazz pianists to play beneath the plane trees and night sky at the Château de Florans.

Chorégies d'Orange show

7 Nice Jazz Festival
MAP Q3 ▪ Jul

Founded in 1948, the best of the region's many jazz festivals draws

3 Chorégies d'Orange
MAP B2 ▪ Jul–early Aug

France's oldest music festival, dating from 1860, has the town's Roman theatre as its main venue (see p125). The original stage wall ensures perfect acoustics that have earned the event an international reputation.

Musician at the Nice Jazz Festival

4 Festival de Quatuors à Cordes
MAP F4 ▪ Jan (every two years)

Celebrated string quartets bring their music to the lovely Gothic, Baroque and Romanesque churches of the perched villages around Fayence – a little-known but moving festival.

some of the biggest names in the music business. The festival sees 32 concerts over 6 nights on two stages in Place Masséna, one concentrating on jazz and the other mixing world music, pop and other genres.

8 Nice Carnival
MAP H4 ▪ Feb

Over 16 days in February, Nice goes wild as multicoloured floats, huge carnival figures and performing troupes take to the streets. Europe's liveliest carnival also features the famous Battle of the Flowers.

Carnival figure in the parade at Nice

9 Fête de la Véraison, Châteauneuf-du-Pape
MAP B3 ▪ 1st weekend Aug

To celebrate the ripening of their grapes, villagers dress in historic costume for three days of parades, medieval crafts and performances.

10 Fête de la Transhumance, St Rémy-de-Provence
MAP B3 ▪ Whitsun weekend

Upwards of 3,000 sheep cram into the old village, for an old-style sheep drive *(transhumance)* to their upland summer pastures. Along with sheep, goats and donkeys are shepherds in traditional costume, food displays and feasting.

TOP 10 SPORTING EVENTS

Monaco Grand Prix

1 Monaco Grand Prix
MAP H3 ▪ May
The one and only street race on the Formula One calendar.

2 Les Voiles de St-Tropez
MAP F5 ▪ Sep–Oct
Six-day regatta for both traditional and modern sailing boats.

3 Pétanque World Championships, Marseille
MAP K4 ▪ Jul
Four days of boules, culminating in a final on the Vieux Port.

4 Olympic Sailing Week, Hyères
MAP E6 ▪ Apr
Some 1,000 boats from 50 nations compete in this sailing event.

5 Feria du Riz, Arles
MAP B4 ▪ Sep
Bullfighting and other festivities welcome the Camargue rice harvest.

6 Paris to Nice "Race to the Sun"
MAP H4 ▪ Mar
Watch the final leg of the international cycling year's first major race.

7 Monte Carlo Tennis Masters
MAP H3 ▪ Apr
One of the tennis circuit's more prestigious events.

8 Olympique de Marseille
The favourite French football team *(see p76)* plays home games July to May.

9 Joûtes Provençales, St Mandrier-sur-Mer
MAP G4 ▪ Jun
An unusual sporting event centred on waterborne jousting.

10 Verdon Canyon Challenge
MAP E3 ▪ Jun
Tough races of 8–100 km (5–62 miles) through this dramatic scenery.

Provence and the Côte d'Azur Area by Area

The perched village of Les-Baux-de-Provence, Bouches-du-Rhône

🔟 Marseille

The Oldest City in France was founded 2,600 years ago by Greek settlers from Asia Minor, and it has barely seen a quiet moment since. Open-hearted and tumultuous, it is backed by chalk hills and flanked by white cliffs, with its face to the sea. The sea is Marseille's

Ceiling of Notre-Dame de la Garde

raison d'être, making it a trading hub and entry point for immigrants. As a result, Marseille is a collection of urban villages, from the souk-like market areas to tiny fishing ports. But all its citizens are *Marseillais*: loud, rebellious and volatile. This is the home of French music, football and *bouillabaisse*. Picaresque and picturesque, it's a place in which to feel alive.

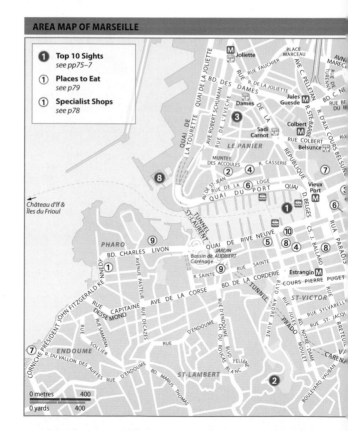

AREA MAP OF MARSEILLE

1. **Top 10 Sights**
   see pp75–7

1. **Places to Eat**
   see p79

1. **Specialist Shops**
   see p78

Château d'If & Îles du Frioul

0 metres   400
0 yards   400

View over Marseille's Vieux Port

1 Vieux Port
MAP K4

Commercial sea traffic might have moved round the corner to newer docks in the 19th century, but the old port remains the heart of city life. Bobbing with boats and fringed with restaurants, it's where the *Marseillais* gather for festivities and buy fish.

The occupying Nazis tried to subdue the city by blowing up the north side of the port in 1943, but Marseille's indomitable nature won the day.

2 Notre-Dame de la Garde
MAP K6 ▪ Rue Forte du Sanctuaire ▪ Open 7am–7:15pm daily (Oct–Mar: to 6:15pm)

This Romanesque-Byzantine church is the symbol of Marseille. Perched on the highest hill and topped by a gold statue of the Virgin, it can be seen from everywhere in the city. Built in the 1850s and restored in the early 2000s, its vaulted crypt is carved out of the rock.

Contemporary interior of MuCEM

3 Museum of Civilizations of Europe and the Mediterranean (MuCEM)
MAP J4 ▪ 7 prom Robert Laffont ▪ Open May–Jun & Sep–Oct: 11am–7pm Wed–Mon (to 6pm in winter); Jul–Aug: 10am–8pm ▪ DA ▪ Adm

This museum is split between a striking postmodernist building on the seafront and the adjacent Fort St-Jean. It features art from around the Mediterranean, from Neolithic times to the present day.

Palais Longchamp fountains

4 Palais Longchamp

MAP M2 ▪ 6 bd de Montricher
▪ Museums: open 10am–6pm
Tue–Sun; closed pub hols; DA; adm
(free Sun)

Longchamp is the greatest expression of Marseille's 19th-century "golden age". What is essentially a water tower is embellished in palatial Second Empire style with fountains, columns and animal sculptures. The central gallery is flanked by two ornate wings, home to the Fine Arts and Natural History museums. Lush gardens stretch behind.

5 Le Panier and Vieille Charité

MAP J3 ▪ La Vieille Charité: 2 rue de la Charité; open 10am–6pm Tue–Sun; closed 1 Jan, 1 May, 1 Nov, 25 Dec; DA; adm

Wriggling up the hill north of the Vieux Port, Le Panier is Marseille's oldest sector. This is where the Greeks settled and, later, where the city's immigrants began their new lives. They still do – the tiny streets are alive with different accents and cultures. La Vieille Charité, the 17th-century workhouse and now a cultural centre, houses the museums of Mediterranean Archaeology and of African, Oceanic and Native American Art. The domed central chapel is Italian Baroque at its purest.

6 Musée Grobet-Labadié

MAP M3 ▪ 140 bd Longchamp
▪ 04 91 62 21 82 (call for details)
▪ Closed for renovation ▪ Adm

Opposite the Palais Longchamp, this museum is set in the former private mansion of a rich 19th-century art-loving Marseille family. Its original decor has been retained, recreating bourgeois life at the peak of the city's prosperity. Walls are hung with a unique collection of Gobelin and Aubusson tapestries, while the salons boast sculpture, paintings, drawings and furniture from the 13th to the 19th centuries.

Painting at Musée Grobet-Labadié

7 Prado Beaches

MAP C5

Around the corniche from the Vieux Port, past the picturesque fishing port of Vallon des Auffes to the start of the *calanques*, stretch Marseille's boldly modern beaches. They were reclaimed from the sea with earth excavated during the building of the city's metro system. On summer days, they feature every conceivable beach sporting activity; at night, the Escale Borély beach area offers some of the town's trendiest nightspots.

8 Les Calanques

MAP C5

Within 15 minutes' drive of the city centre you are out of town and into a

THE FOOTBALL CAPITAL

Champions of Europe, then enmeshed in match-fixing scandals: the recent history of the Olympique de Marseille football team has matched the turbulence of its home town. But this has done nothing to dissuade the fans of the most popular French team – football is the lifeblood of Marseille, the Stade Vélodrome its place of worship.

different world. White rocks plunge into the blue sea and the road winds into inlets *(calanques)* of great beauty. This is where the *Marseillais* spend their weekends, eating, drinking and keeping rich developers out. After Les Goudes, access to even more picturesque creeks (towards Cassis) is by foot or boat only *(see p54)*.

Imposing walls of the Château d'If

⑨ Château d'If
MAP C5 ■ Open Apr–Sep: 10am–6pm daily; Oct–Mar: 10am–5pm Tue–Sun ■ Ferry from Vieux Port ■ Adm

This offshore island fortress was built in the 16th century to protect the city's port and was turned into a prison in 1634. Among its inmates were the real Comte de Mirabeau, and Alexandre Dumas' fictional Count of Monte Cristo *(see p41)*.

⑩ Musée des Arts Décoratifs, de la Faïence et de la Mode
MAP C5 ■ 134 av Clôt Bey ■ Open 10am–6pm Tue–Sun ■ Closed 1 Jan, 1 May, 1 Nov, 25 Dec ■ Adm

Château Borély, a masterpiece of 18th-century architecture, houses exhibition space devoted to decorative arts and furniture; earthenware, ceramics and glass; and fashion from the 17th century to the present day. It brings together collections formerly scattered between the Musée de la Faïence, Musée Cantini and the Musée de Vieux Marseille, along with the furniture collection of the Château itself. The gardens host outdoor exhibitions and concerts.

A MORNING EXPLORING MARSEILLE

Start your day off at the lush and pleasant **Parc Longchamp** (metro Cinq Avenues-Longchamp) for a stroll through the gardens, zoo and the museums of the **Palais Longchamp**, and perhaps also the **Musée Grobet-Labdadié**, just across from the park entrance.

From here you can walk towards the centre on the leafy **boulevard Longchamp** (or better yet take the very stylish and popular new T2 tram) to **boulevard Garibaldi**; walk one block south to **rue du Marché des Capucins**, colourful heart of the city's souk market area (also known as the Marché de Noailles; closed Sun).

When you're done with browsing, follow this street eastwards and turn right into **cours Julien**, a lively centre for musicians and artists, full of alternative bars and street art. From the end of the cours, take rue d'Aubagne north and then left into rue Estelle. Here the style heats up quickly, with the designer shops in and around **rue St Ferréol**.

Where rue Estelle becomes rue Grignan, visit the **Musée Cantini** (open 10am–6pm Tue–Sun; closed pub hols; adm), which houses a magnificent Modernist collection of Fauvist, Cubist and Surrealist paintings.

Rue Paradis brings you to the **Vieux Port**. End your morning stroll at place Thiars, a hive of galleries, restaurants and bars. You will have more than earned your lunchtime *bouillabaisse* at **Le Caribou** *(see p79)*.

See map on pp74–5 ←

Specialist Shops

1 G Bataille
MAP L4 ▪ 25 pl Notre-Dame-du-Mont

Finest grocery-cum-delicatessen in Marseille, with irresistible selections of cheese, cold meats, spices, wines and much more besides.

2 Rue de la Tour
MAP K4

Not one shop but a collection of stores in a tiny street. Here, some of Marseille's leading fashion creators congregate, among them Manon Martin, Zenane and Casablanca.

Stylish boutique in Rue de la Tour

3 Casablanca
MAP L4 ▪ 63 cours Julien
▪ www.boutiquecasablanca.com

One of the arbiters of trendy Marseille style, featuring colourful, comfortable women's clothing.

4 Maison Empereur
MAP L4 ▪ 4 rue des Récollettes
▪ Closed Sun ▪ www.empereur.fr

France's oldest hardware shop, founded in 1827, is a quirky, beloved institution. It sells novel kitchen and household goods, leather, toys and almost anything else you can think of.

5 La Chocolatière de Marseille
MAP K4 ▪ 35 rue Vacon

This tiny establishment makes the best chocolate in the city. Specialities include the mouthwatering *Barre Marseillaise*, made in a wide range of flavours, such as orange and praline.

6 Galeries Lafayette
MAP K4 ▪ Centre Commercial Bourse

The largest store in town is a one-stop shop (clothes, gifts, wines, groceries and more) for those with less time to spare.

7 La Part des Anges
MAP K5 ▪ 33 rue Sainte

Not only a good wine shop and delicatessen but also a restaurant and sophisticated takeaway outlet. It is open every night until 2am.

8 Le Four des Navettes
MAP J5 ▪ 136 rue Sainte

The oldest bakery in town and, since 1781, home of the traditional Marseillais *navette*, a small biscuit (cookie) flavoured with orange blossom and, aptly for this port city, shaped like a boat.

9 Dromel Ainé
MAP L6 ▪ 19 av Prado

Even older than the above, Dromel Ainé has been in the business of selling fantastic chocolates, sweets, and a range of unusual teas and coffees since 1760. An unmissable Marseille experience.

10 Boutique de Compagnie de Provence-Marseille
MAP J4 ▪ 1 rue Caisserie

Not far from the Vieux Port, this shop sells authentic olive oil *savon de Marseille* in all its forms, plus scented candles and diffusers.

Compagnie de Provence-Marseille

Places to Eat

PRICE CATEGORIES
For a three-course meal for one with half
a bottle of wine (or equivalent meal),
taxes and extra charges.

€ under €40 €€ €40–€60 €€€ over €60

1 Restaurant Chez Michel
MAP J5 = 6 rue des Catalans
= 04 91 52 30 63 = DA = €€€

Chez Michel is known for serving
the finest *bouillabaisse* in town, as
well as several other traditional
Marseillaise seafood specialities.
It overlooks Catalan beach.

2 Dayo
MAP J4 = 40 rue Caisserie
= 04 91 93 13 37 = Closed Mon = €€

This a favourite with locals and
visitors alike for its delicious seafood
and steaks grilled on the *plancha*.

3 Les Arcenaulx
MAP K5 = 25 cours Honoré
d'Estienne d'Orves = 04 91 59 80 30
= Closed Sun = €€

Dine in the extraordinary setting
of the former 17th-century arsenal,
complete with atmospheric vaults.
Besides the regional restaurant,
there is a bookshop and a boutique.

4 La Table du Fort
MAP K5 = 8 rue Fort Notre
Dame = 04 91 33 97 65 = Closed Sun,
Sat–Mon L = €€

A welcoming husband-and-wife
team consistently serve inventive
contemporary cuisine made using
local produce. The restaurant is just
a few steps from the Vieux Port.

5 L'Epuisette
MAP C5 = Vallon des Auffes
= 04 91 52 17 82 = Closed Sun, Mon
= €€€

Set amid Marseille's traditional
seaside cabins, L'Epuisette has
splendid views from its dining area.
Fresh fish, along with other local
produce, is prepared and served in a
range of exquisite modern dishes.

Plateau de fruits de mer at Chez Toinou

6 Chez Toinou
MAP L4 = 3 cours St Louis
= 04 91 33 14 94 = Closed Sun, Mon
= DA = €€

One of the best – and cheapest –
places for seafood in Marseille.
Those willing to share can savour a
plateau de fruits de mer for about €18
per person; for more traditional
types, there's mussels and chips.

7 Le Souk
MAP J4 = 98 quai du Port = 04
91 91 29 29 = Closed Mon = DA = €

Great Moroccan food in a lovely
setting with a view of the cathedral.

8 29 Place aux Huiles
MAP K5 = 29 pl aux Huiles
= 04 91 33 26 44 = Closed Sun D = €€

Dishes change with the seasons
here, but there is always something
interesting on the menu.

9 Les Trois Forts
MAP J5 = Hôtel Sofitel du
Vieux-Port, 36 bd Charles-Livon
= 04 91 15 59 56 = DA = €€€

Great views over the port accompany
sumptuous seafood dishes.

10 Le Caribou
MAP K5 = 38 pl Thiars = 04 91
33 22 63 = Closed Sun, Mon, Jun–Sep
= DA = €€

First-rate fish and game has been
served here since 1945.

See map on pp74–5 ←

🔟 Bouches-du-Rhône

The Bouches-du-Rhône region is aptly named (*bouches* means mouths), for here the river splits into several separate streams, flowing into the Mediterranean via the lagoons and grassy plains of the Camargue. The Rhône marks Provence's western boundary and for centuries it was the region's highway. Many important towns grew up along its banks, while villages and medieval abbeys nestle in the hills. Windswept beaches fringe the Camargue, but east of the delta the coast becomes rocky, with small inlets (*calanques*).

Flamingoes in the Camargue

AREA MAP OF BOUCHES-DU-RHÔNE

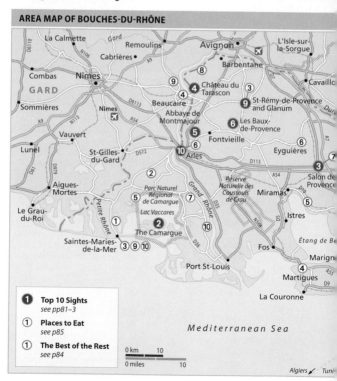

1 Top 10 Sights
see pp81–3

① Places to Eat
see p85

① The Best of the Rest
see p84

Fountain in Aix-en-Provence

1 Aix-en-Provence

Aix is just a stone's throw from the sprawl of Marseille, but keeps its own identity, with cosmopolitan cafés, a grand cathedral and beautiful 18th-century fountains (see pp18–19).

2 The Camargue

This vast expanse of wetlands, salt marshes, lagoons and grazing land, home to a range of rare bird and animal species, is protected within the Parc Naturel Régional de Camargue and other conservation areas (see pp26–7).

3 Salon de Provence
MAP C4

Salon, one of the oldest villages in Provence, is today a busy modern town, host to the French Air Force training school. The old town, sitting on a hill, has an attractive historic centre, with medieval buildings, quiet streets and leafy, café-lined squares. The main attraction is the Château de l'Empéri (see p84) dating from the 10th century. Other places to visit include the small museum dedicated to Nostradamus, who lived here in the 16th century, and the Musée de Savon at Savonnerie Fabre, which bears witness to the olive oil industry which has existed here for over 600 years.

Château de Tarascon

4 Château de Tarascon
MAP B3 ■ Bd du Roi René, Tarascon ■ Open Feb–May & Oct: 9:30am–5:30pm daily (Jun–Sep: to 6:30pm; Nov–Jan: to 5pm) ■ Closed public hols ■ Adm

The pale battlements of the Château de Tarascon seem straight from a historical romance. Built to guard a vital Rhône crossing on Provence's borders, the castle has steep, crenellated curtain walls between massive round towers. It was begun by King Louis of Anjou, ruler of Provence in the 15th century, and was completed by his successor, King René. On his death, Provence became part of France (see p37) and the castle lost its strategic importance, becoming a prison until 1926.

(5) Abbaye de Montmajour
MAP B4 ▪ Rte de Fontvieille,
Arles ▪ Open Apr–May: 10am–5pm
daily; Jun–Sep: 10am–6:30pm daily;
Oct–Mar: 10am–5pm Tue–Sun
▪ Closed 1 Jan, 1 May, 1 & 11 Nov,
25 Dec ▪ Adm

This massive, fortress-like abbey was
built by Benedictine monks in the 10th
century. Then, the low hill on which it
stands was an island surrounded by
marshes and is still known as Mount
Ararat. Damaged by fire in 1726, it
was restored in the 19th century, and
its Église Notre-Dame is one of the
largest Romanesque buildings in
Provence. Below the church, a 12th-
century crypt and chapel have been
carved into the hillside (see p47).

Abbaye de Montmajour

(6) Les-Baux-de-Provence
MAP B4 ▪ Château des Baux:
Open daily; Mar, Oct: 9:30am–6:30pm;
Apr–Jun, Sep: 9am–7pm; Jul, Aug:
9am–8pm; Nov–Feb: 10am–6pm; Adm

Perched on a limestone crag, Les
Baux is one of the most dramatic
fortified villages in Provence. It is
crowned by a ruined château with
walls that date from the 10th century.
Église St-Vincent has 20th-century
stained glass by Max Ingrand. The
village is closed to cars (see p48).

BLACK BULLS AND WHITE HORSES

The wild black bulls of the Camargue
are one of the symbols of Bouches-du-
Rhône, along with white horses –
direct descendants of the prehistoric
wild horse of Europe. These are still
ridden by the *gardians*, the sombrero-
wearing cowboys of the Camargue.

Château and harbour of Cassis

(7) Cassis
MAP D5

This pretty fishing port (see p49) with
its brightly coloured fishing boats
anchored in a harbour on a rugged,
rocky coastline, was a favourite with
painters such as Dufy, Derain and
Matisse (see pp40–41), all of whom
were inspired by its clear light and
Mediterranean hues. Amazingly, it
has escaped being spoiled by tourism.
Cassis is also noted for its excellent
seafood (fresh sea urchins are
considered a local delicacy) and
there are plenty of good restaurants.

(8) Abbaye de Silvacane
MAP C4 ▪ La Roque d'Anthéron
▪ Open: Apr–May: 10am–1pm,
2–5:30pm Tue–Sun; Jun–Sep: 10am–
6pm daily; Oct–Mar: 10am–1pm,
2–5pm Tue–Sun ▪ Adm

Along with Sénanque (see pp30–31)
and Thoronet, Silvacane is one of the
three great sister-abbeys built in the
12th century by the Cistercian order
as it rose to prominence in Provence.
Its plain, austere architecture reflects
the rule of the order, which was
founded by St Bernard in protest
at the luxury and corruption of other
monasteries. The church has a high,
vaulted transept and the cloister
arcades and refectory were added
in the 13th and 14th centuries.
Abandoned by its monks in the late
14th century, it became a living
abbey once again in the 20th century.

9 St Rémy-de-Provence and Glanum

MAP B3 ■ Musée des Alpilles: pl Favier, St-Rémy; open May–Sep: 10am–6pm Tue–Sun (Jul–Aug: to 10pm Tue); Oct–Apr: 1–5:30pm Tue–Sat; Closed 1 Jan, 1 May, 25 Dec; Adm

Overlooked by the wooded, limestone hills of Les Alpilles, St-Rémy is a perfect exploring base. Mansions built in the 15th and 16th centuries grace its historic centre. One of them was the original home of the de Sade family, ancestors of the notorious Marquis. It houses the small Musée des Alpilles, displaying artifacts found at Glanum, about 30 minutes' walk from the town centre. Here, the site of one of the most ancient Greek-Roman settlements in Provence is marked by a magnificent triumphal arch and mausoleum (see p43).

10 Roman Arles

The delightful town of Arles, founded by the Romans, stands on the east bank of the Rhône and is the gateway to Provence from the west (see pp16–17).

Les Arènes, Arles

Start the day with a visit to the largest and most striking Roman monument in Provence, **Les Arènes** (see p16). From the highest tier of seats you have a fine view of the historic centre and the Rhône. From here, walk across to the **Théâtre Antique** (see p16), for another glimpse of Roman Arles, then walk down the rue du Cloître to the place de la République, where water gushes from bronze masks at the foot of an obelisk, brought here from Egypt by the Romans.

On the east side of the square, visit the fine Romanesque **Église St-Trophime** (see p16), with its lovely sculpted pillars crowned by little figures of saints and martyrs. Follow the rue de l'Hôtel de Ville to **Les Thermes de Constantin** (see p16), the remains of a palace built for a 4th-century AD Roman emperor. Then spend up to an hour in the **Musée Réattu** (rue du Grand-Prieuré; open Tue–Sun; adm), with its fine collection of art from the 18th to 20th centuries, including works by Picasso.

Another great painter, Van Gogh, is associated with Place du Forum, which is cluttered with cafés – one has been painted to look just as it was in his work Café la Nuit. Stop in for coffee. End the morning at the **Fondation Vincent van Gogh Arles** (35 rue du Dr Fanton; open Apr–Sep: 11am–7pm daily; Oct–Mar: 11am–6pm Tue–Sun; adm), which features contemporary works highlighting Van Gogh's influence on 20th- and 21st-century artists.

See map on pp80–81 ←

The Best of the Rest

1 Parc Ornithologique du Pont-de-Gau, the Camargue

MAP A4 ■ Open 9am–7pm daily (Oct–Mar: 10am–6pm) ■ Adm

For a superb view of the Camargue, visit the bird park, where enclosures display the lagoons' bird life (see p27).

2 Musée de la Camargue

MAP B4 ■ Mas du Pont de Rousty, Arles ■ Open Apr–Sep: 9am–12:30pm, 1–6pm Wed–Mon; Oct–Mar: 10am–12:30pm, 1–5pm Wed–Mon ■ Closed Jan, 1 May, 25 Dec ■ Adm

The Camargue comes to life in this fascinating museum (see p26).

3 Église de Notre-Dame, Les-Saintes-Maries-de-la-Mer

MAP A4 ■ Pl de l'Église ■ Open 3–6pm daily (Dec–Mar: Sat & Sun only) ■ Adm

Dominating the seaside village, this 12th-century church (see p47) houses relics of St Sara and has a 4th-century BC taurobolium altar.

4 Château de Beaucaire

MAP B3 ■ Pl Raymond VII ■ Open Apr–Sep: 9:30am–6pm, Wed–Sat, 10am–6pm Sun; Oct–Mar: 8:30am–5pm Wed–Sat, 10am–5pm Sun ■ Adm for tower only

This ruined 11th-century castle faces the Château de Tarascon (see p81).

5 Pont Flavien

MAP B4

Near the village of St-Chamas, this Roman bridge, from the reign of Augustus in the 1st century AD, has beautifully preserved triumphal arches at both ends (see p43).

6 Eyguières

MAP C4

This village was the source of Arles's water supply in Roman times, via an aqueduct. A 12th-century chapel, a 17th-century church and a ruined castle stand in the village.

7 Château de l'Empéri, Salon-de-Provence

MAP C4 ■ Montée du Puech ■ Open mid-Apr–Sep: 9:30am–noon, 2–6pm Tue–Sun; Oct–mid-Apr: 1:30–6pm Tue–Sun ■ Closed pub hols ■ Adm

This imposing 9th-century château was once the seat of the archbishops of Arles. It now houses a fascinating museum of military history.

8 Abbaye de St-Michel de Frigolet

MAP B3 ■ Open 10:15am–12:15pm, 2–6pm daily ■ Adm for tours on Sun

The most attractive aspect of this 19th-century abbey is its painted depictions of saints.

9 Abbaye de St-Roman

MAP B3 ■ Open Apr–mid-Oct: 10am–1pm, 2–6:30pm Tue pm–Sun (Jul & Aug: to 7pm daily); mid-Oct–Mar: 2–5:30pm Tue–Sun (Mar: to 6:30pm) ■ Closed Mon, 25 Dec ■ Adm

This remarkable 5th-century abbey, carved into a rock face, is the only troglodyte monastery in Europe.

10 Musée du Riz, Sambuc

MAP B4 ■ Rizerie du Petit Manusclat ■ Closed for renovation until 2017 ■ Adm

This rice museum sits in the midst of the Camargue paddy fields. Guided tours finish with the tasting of a dish made using the local rice.

Château de Beaucaire

Places to Eat

1 L'Esprit de la Violette, Aix-en-Provence

MAP C4 ▪ 10 av Violette ▪ 04 42 23 02 50 ▪ Closed Sun, Mon ▪ €€€

Michelin-starred Chef Marc de Passorio delights discerning diners with his elegant, refined and creative cuisine. The weekday lunchtime set menu is good value.

Interior of L'Esprit de la Violette

2 La Bastide du Cours, Aix-en-Provence

MAP C4 ▪ 43 cours Mirabeau ▪ 04 42 26 10 06 ▪ €

Slow-roasted Provençal lamb is one of the many treats on offer at this terracotta-toned hotel-restaurant.

3 La Cuisine des Anges, St-Rémy-de-Provence

MAP B3 ▪ 4 rue 8 mai 1945 ▪ 04 90 92 17 66 ▪ Closed Thu; Mon, Tue & Fri L & Sun D; Feb & Mar: Mon–Thu; Jan ▪ DA ▪ €

The restaurant at this B&B, Le Sommeil des Fées, is a local favourite for lamb tagine and Provençal classics.

4 Le Garage, Martigues

MAP C5 ▪ 20 av Frédéric Mistral ▪ 04 42 44 09 51 ▪ Closed Sun, Mon, Aug, 2 wks Jan ▪ DA ▪ €€

Chef Fabien Morreale cooks refined fusion dishes in an Art Deco garage.

5 Le Mazet du Vaccarès, Arles

MAP B4 ▪ D37, rte Albaron Villeneuve ▪ 04 90 97 10 79 ▪ Closed mid-Jan–Feb ▪ No credit cards ▪ No vegetarian options ▪ DA ▪ €€

Located on the edge of the Étang de Vaccarès, this is the place to sample Camargue clams in lemon cream. Open Friday lunch to Sunday lunch.

6 Le Jardin de Manon, Arles

MAP B4 ▪ 4 av Alyscamps ▪ 04 90 93 38 68 ▪ Closed Tue & Sun D, Wed ▪ DA ▪ €€

Enjoy scrumptious dishes such as roast duck, rabbit or *sole meunière* in a lovely garden setting.

7 La Chassagnette, Arles

MAP B4 ▪ Rte du Sambuc ▪ 04 90 97 26 96 ▪ Closed Tue, Wed, mid-Dec–Mar ▪ DA ▪ €€€

Chef Armand Arnal uses organic vegetables from the farm's garden in his dishes. Pick your own herbs for a digestive *tisane* at the end of the meal.

8 Le Bistro Latin, Aix-en-Provence

MAP C4 ▪ 18 rue de la Couronne ▪ 04 42 38 22 88 ▪ Closed Sun, Mon D, Wed L ▪ €

This bistro is fun, informal and famous for its scallop risotto.

9 El Campo, Saintes-Maries-de-la-Mer

MAP A4 ▪ 13 rue Victor Hugo ▪ 04 90 97 84 11 ▪ Closed Sun D, Mon, Feb–early Mar ▪ DA ▪ €€

Wash down a bull-meat casserole with a glass of Costières de Nîmes, listening to live gypsy flamenco.

10 A Fleur de Sel, Saintes-Maries-de-la-Mer

MAP A4 ▪ 43 rue Frédéric Mistral ▪ 04 90 97 83 42 ▪ Closed Wed ▪ €€

A great place to go for fresh seafood platters and grilled fish, Camargue beef and decadent desserts.

See map on pp80–81 ←

TOP 10 The Var and Provençal Coast

Within just a 30-minute drive of the glamour of St-Tropez, you can be on a rugged mountainside so remote that you may dread nightfall. That's the charm of the Var – an intoxicating mix of the good life and an untamed landscape. In the Gorges du Verdon and Upper Var, nature is both wild and imposing; down below, on the coast, beauty assumes more rounded forms in beach resorts and casinos. Yet the Provençal tendency to "let time take its time" unites the region. Little wonder that this is the most popular of French holiday regions.

Carvings, Basilica St-Maximin

AREA MAP OF THE VAR AND PROVENÇAL COAST

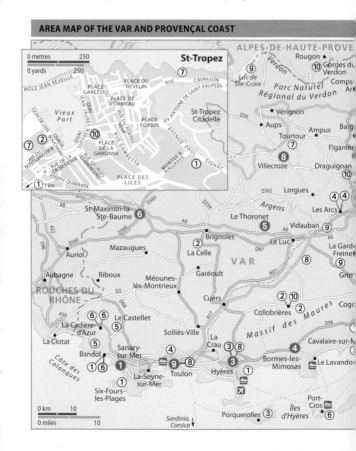

Sanary-sur-Mer harbour

1 Sanary-sur-Mer
MAP D5

The prettiest harbour in the Var remains a proper fishing port, bobbing with boats. Beyond, palm trees fringe a frontage of pastel façades. Activities range from

relaxed to intense, notably during the morning market which enlivens the Allées d'Estienne-d'Orves. Look for plaques commemorating Thomas Mann, Bertolt Brecht and other German writers who took refuge from the Nazis here in the 1930s.

2 Fréjus Old Town
MAP F5 ■ Cathédrale St-Léonce: open 10am–12:30pm & 1:45–6:30pm daily (Oct–May: 10am–1pm, 2–5pm Tue–Sun); closed 1 Jan, 1 May, 1 & 11 Nov, 25 Dec; adm (cloisters only)

Despite its relaxed image, Fréjus has an exceptional double heritage. As Forum Julii, it was the second port of the Roman Empire in the region and retains some of the oldest and most extensive remains in Provence. Particularly notable are the elliptical, 12,000-seater arena and theatre (see p42). Meanwhile, the town's medieval bishopric status has left it with an extraordinary group of episcopal buildings. The 13th-century cathedral incorporates a wonderful octagonal baptistry from an earlier, 5th-century church, while the 14th-century cloisters have ceilings painted with bracingly lurid events from the Apocalypse (see p47).

Baptistry at Cathédrale St-Léonce

3 Villa Noailles, Hyères
MAP E6 ■ Montée Noailles ■ 04 98 08 01 98 ■ Closed Jul–Sep: Tue; Oct–Jun: Mon & Tue

Built between 1923 and 1927 for avant-garde art patrons Charles and Marie-Laure de Noailles, this Cubist villa hosts changing exhibits on design, photography, fashion and modern architecture.

Map legend (within img_4):

Var

ALPES-MARITIMES

Gréolières
Gourdon
Mons
Saint-Vallier-de-Thiey
eillans
Grasse
Fayence
Mougins
Lac de St-Cassien
Mandelieu-la-Napoule
Cannes
Bagnols-en-Forêt
luy
Massif de l'Esterel
Îles de Lérins
Fréjus
St-Raphaël
Côte de l'Esterel
Mediterranean Sea
see St-Tropez map, left
mutuelle

Hilltop village of Bormes-les-Mimosas

④ Bormes-les-Mimosas
MAP E5

This is a glorious village, unravelling down the hillside in a cascade of little streets, stairways, terracotta-tiled rooftops and flowers *(see p49)*.

⑤ Abbaye du Thoronet, Le Thoronet
MAP E4 ▪ Quai Abbaye ▪ Open 10am–6:30pm Mon–Sat; 10am–noon, 2–6:30pm Sun (Oct–Mar: 10am–1pm, 2–5pm Mon–Sat, 10am–noon, 2–5pm Sun) ▪ Closed 1 Jan, 1 May, 1 & 11 Nov, 25 Dec ▪ Adm

This majestic 12th-century Cistercian abbey was built in a wooded dip near Lorgues. Probably the finest example of Romanesque architecture in the region, along with its sister houses, Silvacane and Sénanque *(see pp30–31)*, it rises with sober magnificence. The un-mortared stones of the church, the monks' buildings and the cloisters are decorated only by changing sunlight, their interior volumes inspiring awe and serenity. The harmony of structure and setting make contemplation unavoidable.

⑥ Basilica St-Maximin, St-Maximin-la-Ste-Baume
MAP D4 ▪ Open 9am–6pm daily (except during Mass)

Provence's finest example of Gothic architecture was erected to house the relics of Mary Magdalene, "discovered" on the site in 1280. The basilica appears unfinished from the outside (there is no belfry) but within, the sense of balance is stunning. So too are the treasures, notably a 16th-century altarpiece depicting the Passion of Christ, and a renowned 17th-century organ. Mary Magdalene's remains are in a reliquary and a marble sarcophagus in the crypt.

⑦ Massif de l'Esterel
MAP G4

As the rugged red rocks of the Esterel range plunge into the blue of the Mediterranean, they create creeks and contrasts of stirring beauty. Inland, the tough, volcanic mountains may rise no higher than 600 m (2,000 ft) but the landscape is of breathtaking gorges, passes and peaks. Many paths and tracks provide access to the mountainscape and its rich tree life. Take the Perthus or tougher Mal-Infernet valleys – in the footsteps of brigands who hid out here *(see p65)*.

Massif de l'Esterel

8. Caves, Villecroze

MAP E4 ■ Open Apr–May:
2–6pm Wed–Sun; Jun & Sep: 10:30am–
12:30pm, 2–6pm Wed–Sun; Jul–Aug:
10:30am–12:30pm, 2–6pm daily
■ Adm

Riddling the wall of rock that
dominates the medieval village, these
caves were first home to prehistoric
people and, later, provided refuge
against Saracen pirates. Most startling,
however, is a cave on the north side of
the village, transformed by a 16th-
century nobleman into a four-storey,
fortified house, with Renaissance
frontage, staircases and windows cut
out of the stone. A spring creates a
cascade which waters gardens below.

Troglodyte caves at Villecroze

9. Toulon

MAP E5 ■ Musée de la Marine:
pl Monsenergue; open 10am–6pm
Wed–Mon; closed Jan; DA; adm

France's biggest, and once gritty,
naval port has made a remarkable
comeback. Explore the spruced-up
old port, take the cable car up Mont
Faron for spectacular views and visit
the outstanding Musée de la Marine.

10. Musée des Arts et Traditions Populaires, Draguignan

MAP F4 ■ 15 rue Joseph Roumanille
■ Open 9am–noon, 2–6pm Tue–Sat
(Apr–Sep: 2–6pm Sun) ■ Closed 1 Jan,
1 May, 25 Dec ■ Adm

Housed in 18th-century buildings in
the old town, this is one of the best
ethnographic museums in France.
Its displays illustrate the story of
Provençal life from its earliest days
to the beginning of the 20th century.

A DAY'S DRIVE IN THE MASSIF DES MAURES

▶ MORNING

Start in the village of **Grimaud**
and take the D558 up to **La
Garde-Freinet** (see p90). Continue
7 km (4 miles) before turning left
(D75) towards Gonfaron and stop
at the **Village des Tortues** to see
the rare native Hermann tortoise
(Quartier Plaine: open 9am–7pm
daily (to 6pm Dec–Feb); adm). Take
the D39 towards Collobrières.
At Col des Fourches head up
to **Notre-Dame des Anges**, the
Maures's highest point. There's a
fascinating chapel and fine views.

About 3 km (2 miles) before
Collobrières, turn left (D14)
to the **Chartreuse de la Verne**,
a 12th-century Carthusian
monastery (Quartier Verne: open
11am–5pm Wed–Mon, adm).
Then double back to **Collobrières**
(see p90). Stop for a drink or lunch
at **La Petite Fontaine** (see p93).

AFTERNOON

Leave towards Pierrefeu, but
2 km (1 mile) later turn left (D41)
towards **Bormes-les-Mimosas**.
The drive, between wooded slopes
and plunging valleys, takes you
over the Col de Babao to the N98.
Turn left towards La Mole, but
stop off at the **Arboretum de
Gratteloup** (N98), a forest garden
with around 50 tree varieties.

Continue to **La Mole**, then turn
right (D27) to the Col du Canadel
and stop at the **Domaine du Rayol**
gardens (see p52). Returning to
Grimaud, enjoy dinner at **Le
Côteau Fleuri** (pl des Pénitents;
04 94 43 20 17; closed Tue; €€).

See map on pp86–7 ←

Var Villages

1 Mons
MAP F4

Almost 820 m (2,700 ft) up, Mons has the heritage to match its grandiose position: remains of the great Roche Taillée Roman aqueduct run nearby. In the village itself, narrow alleys wind around ancient porches, pretty arcades and the wonderful 12th-century church.

2 Collobrières
MAP E5

It's difficult to resist a village claiming to be "world capital of candied chestnuts". In the heart of the Massif des Maures *(see p89)*, Collobrières is surrounded by forested slopes.

3 Ramatuelle
MAP F5

Although swamped by the overspill from St-Tropez in summer, Ramatuelle remains a lovely hilltop village. Its tiny streets and vaulted passages are heavy with flowers.

4 Les Arcs-sur-Argens
MAP F4

With the medieval castle up top, the rest of the old village hugs the rocky promontory. Its labyrinth of streets and vaulted stairways unfold to the modern village below.

5 Le Castellet
MAP D5

The only access to this glorious perched village is via two gates in its 13th-century walls. Within, steep paved streets climb tortuously to the feudal castle. Views over olive groves to the sea are outstanding.

Perched village of Le Castellet

6 La Cadière-d'Azur
MAP D5

The medieval St-Jean gate is a great introduction to this ravishing maze of streets set above the terraced hillsides and vineyards of Bandol. The panorama is breathtaking.

7 Tourtour
MAP F4

Remote, perched at 600 m (2,000 ft) up and surrounded by pine forest, Tourtour is a picturesque tangle of streams, medieval buildings and old stone streets leading to a main square lined with restaurants.

8 Comps-sur-Artuby
MAP F4

This is high, wild country, where the Knights Templar made a base. The 12th-century St-André chapel testifies to their presence, and affords unbeatable views over the nearby Artuby Gorges.

9 La Garde-Freinet
MAP F5

Nestling amid forests of cork-oak and chestnut, La Garde-Freinet stands sentry to the wild Maures Mountains. Higher still are the ruins of the medieval village fortified by Saracens.

10 Callas
MAP F4

Fortified on the side of a green hill, Callas has a winding, self-contained charm imposed by its isolation near the edge of the Canjuers Plateau. It's also a fine base for walking the nearby Pennafort Gorges.

Sporting and Outdoor Activities

1 Watersports
The Var coast offers everything, from sailing and tuna-fishing to windsurfing and parascending. Resorts awarded the "Station Voile" symbol for excellent watersports facilities include Hyères and Bandol. Meanwhile, Brutal Beach at Six-Fours draws international windsurfers (see p65) and Cavalaire claims to be the French capital of jet-skiing.

Windsurfing at Cavalaire

2 Hill Walks in the Maures Mountains
The walking possibilities amid these forests, valleys and peaks (see p89) are magnificent. The two-hour Collobrières to Chartreuse de la Verne monastery trek is one of the best.

3 Cycling on Porquerolles
Cars are banned on the island of Porquerolles, so cycling is the most rewarding way to explore it. Hire bikes from the village (see p54).

4 Mont Faron
MAP E5
Rising up 540 m (2,000 ft) behind the city of Toulon, Mont Faron is most dramatically reached by cable car from boulevard Admiral Vence. The views and walks are terrific.

5 Golf
MAP D5 ■ Golf de Frégate, Route de Bandol, St Cyr-sur-Mer
The Var has a dozen golf courses, of which the best-known is the Golf de Frégate, set among vineyards and olive groves and overlooking the sea.

6 Scuba Marine Park, Port-Cros
MAP F6 ■ Tourist office: 04 94 01 40 70
An underwater guided path. Hire flippers, snorkel and a mask, make for Le Palud beach and follow the buoys to discover posidonia, coral, mother-of-pearl and brightly coloured fish. It is vital that you call the tourist office before setting out.

7 Coastal Walk, St-Tropez
MAP F5
Far from the crowds, the path winds around creeks and beaches, offering lovely views. From Graniers beach to Cap Camarat takes 6 hours.

8 Formula One Driving
MAP E5 ■ AGS Formule 1, Circuit du Var, Gonfaron ■ 04 94 60 97 00
Try the one-day course, open to all drivers at the Le Luc circuit. Expensive but undeniably thrilling.

9 Sailing, Lac de Ste-Croix
MAP E3
This vast artificial lake (see p15) offers all sorts of boating, from pedalo to dinghy. It's also an access point for canoe trips up the gorges.

Mountain biking, Gorges du Verdon

10 Mountain Biking
Tough trail cyclists are spoiled for choice in the Var. The most dramatic trips are around the Gorges du Verdon (see pp14–15) but Draguignan, Figanières and Fréjus also provide challenging routes.

See map on pp86–7 ←

Var Nightlife

1 Les Caves du Roy, St-Tropez
MAP F5 ■ Av Paul Signac ■ www.lescavesduroy.com

The Byblos Hotel's legendary club has a suitably strict door policy: the unfashionable are generally unfortunate. Once selected, you're at the heart of Tropezien nightlife (see p58).

2 L'Opèra, St-Tropez
MAP F5 ■ Rte Residence du Port

This pillar of the resort's jet-set nightlife since 1962 has a waterfront cabaret-restaurant with an all-white dining room. In the evening, enjoy performances on the central stage by flame-throwers, exotic dancers and violin players.

3 Casino des Palmiers, Hyères
MAP E6 ■ Av Ambroise Thomas

Renovated in the 1990s, the casino has retained its belle époque style, added on a glass dome and widened its horizons. Alongside the gaming rooms are a hotel, restaurant and nightclub.

4 La Rhumerie, Cavalaire-Sur-Mer
MAP F5 ■ Rue du Port

This lively cocktail bar, with frequent live bands and theme nights, rocks the seaside until late.

5 Camino, St-Raphaël
MAP F5 ■ Port Santa-Lucia

Sip a rum cocktail while you salsa, mambo and merengue the night away. There are musical dinners from Thursday to Saturday, plus Sunday brunch and afternoon garden parties.

6 Casino Partouche, Bandol
MAP D5 ■ Pl Lucien Artaud

A stylish spot in which to play the fruit machines, the tables – or the field. The complex also boasts a reputable restaurant and sleek lounge bar, both with great views.

7 VIP Room, St-Tropez
MAP F5 ■ Résidence du Nouveau Port

A Studio 54-like vibe prevails at this exclusive supper/dance club. If you're not eating, don't bother turning up before midnight, which is when the trendy set arrives.

8 L'Arbe a Bulles, Toulon
MAP E5 ■ 7 rue Jean Aicard

Toulon's favourite bar is tiny, filled with second-hand furniture, and attracts a very trendy crowd from cocktail hour until late.

Trendy interior at L'Arbe a Bulles

9 The Tube, Saint-Laurent-du-Var
MAP G4 ■ 15 av Docteur Robin

Unlike the nightclubs of St-Tropez, there are no bouncers at this club and restaurant by the Port du Plaisance, where the DJ spins all the latest hits.

10 Bar du Port, St-Tropez
MAP F5 ■ 7 quai Suffren

This high-tech bar on the port starts early (open for breakfast at 7am) and closes late (4am). The rhythm changes as the day goes by, with lunch and dinner served before DJ-driven house music kicks in.

Places to Eat

PRICE CATEGORIES
For a three-course meal for one with half
a bottle of wine (or equivalent meal),
taxes and extra charges.
....
€ under €40   €€ €40–€60   €€€ over €60

① Les Viviers du Pilon, St-Tropez

MAP F5 ■ 2 av Général-de-Gaulle
■ 04 94 97 00 92 ■ Closed Wed,
Nov–Mar ■ €€

Next to a fishmonger's overlooking
the Golfe, this sunny restaurant
offers some of the freshest seafood
on the coast: the seared tuna with
home-made pesto is sublime.

② Hostellerie de l'Abbaye de La Celle, La Celle

MAP F5 ■ 10 pl du Général-de-Gaulle
■ 04 98 05 14 14 ■ Closed Jan, Tue &
Wed in winter ■ DA ■ €€€

Chef Nicolas Pierantoni serves
exquisite Provençal fare using
produce from the organic vegetable
garden of this 18th-century inn.

③ Café des Jardiniers, Le Rayol-Canadel

MAP F5 ■ Le Domaine du Rayol, av
des Belges ■ 04 98 04 44 00 ■ Closed
2 weeks Jan, D ■ DA ■ €

Enjoy a lunch of soup, omelette and
salads, using fresh produce from
these lovely waterside gardens just
west of St-Tropez.

④ Le Logis du Guetteur, Les Arcs-sur-Argens

MAP F4 ■ Pl du Château ■ 04 94 99 51
10 ■ Closed mid-Feb–mid-Mar ■ €€€

This 11th-century castle is now a
superb restaurant. In winter, dine
from the old lookout tower; in
summer, eat al fresco on the terrace.

⑤ La Brasserie, St-Raphaël

MAP F5 ■ 6 av de Valescune ■
04 94 95 25 00 ■ Closed Sun, Jan ■ €

This hidden gem serves French
cuisine on a garden terrace shaded
by lemon and magnolia trees.

⑥ Hostellerie Bérard, La Cadière-d'Azur

MAP D5 ■ 6 rue Gabriel Péri ■ 04 94
90 11 43 ■ Closed Mon, Tue, mid Jan–
early Feb ■ DA ■ €€€

A former monastery offers distinctly
non-monastic standards of luxury
and innovative Provençal cuisine.

Breakfast at Hostellerie Bérard

⑦ La Pomme de Pin, Ramatuelle

MAP F5 ■ Rte de Tahiti ■ 04 94 97 73
70 ■ Closed mid-Oct–Mar ■ €

Mouthwatering Sardinian cuisine in a
convivial setting. Try the *culurgiones*,
filled with fresh sheep's cheese.

⑧ L'Acquaresto, Hyères

MAP E6 ■ 44 av Alphonse
Denis ■ 04 94 65 75 72 ■ Closed Sun,
Mon–Thu D ■ €

Fresh, contemporary cuisine at good
prices has made this a new local
favourite. Save room for dessert.

⑨ La Bastide des Magnans, Vidauban

MAP F5 ■ 32 av Maréchal Galliéni
■ 04 94 99 43 91 ■ Closed Mon ■ DA
■ €€€

La Bastide takes the simplest local
ingredients and comes up with a
balanced array of wonderful tastes.

⑩ La Petite Fontaine, Collobrières

MAP E5 ■ Pl de la République ■ 04 94
48 00 12 ■ Closing times vary, call in
advance ■ No credit cards ■ €

Excellent, no-frills regional cooking
in a characterful village restaurant.

See map on pp86–7

TOP 10 Nice

Nice – the very name sparkles with sunlight and glamour. In the 19th century, the European aristocracy colonized the place, drawn by the glorious Bay of Angels and the mild winter weather. Artists such as Matisse and Chagall were inspired by Nice's limpid light and left their mark here *(see pp40–41)*. Millionaires and film stars would soon follow. There is another Nice, however, rooted in Mediterranean history. For centuries part of the kingdom of Savoy, Nice voted to join France only in 1860, and retains its own dialect and traditions. It is a combination of all this that makes Nice so attractive to a new generation of creative types, who in recent years have made the city livelier than ever.

Cathédrale St-Nicolas

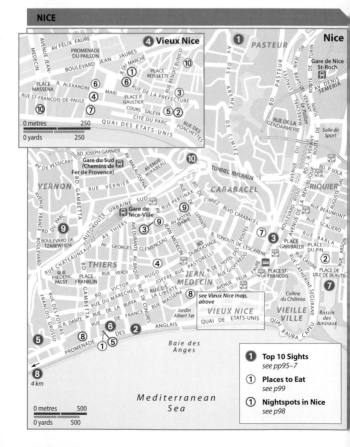

NICE

- ① Top 10 Sights
  see pp95–7
- ① Places to Eat
  see p99
- ① Nightspots in Nice
  see p98

1 Musée Matisse

MAP Q1 ■ 164 av des Arènes de Cimiez ■ Open 10am–6pm Wed–Mon ■ Closed 1 Jan, Easter, 1 May, 25 Dec ■ Adm

Shortly before his death in 1954, Henri Matisse (see p41) donated a collection of paintings to the city he had lived in for 37 years. They have found a superb home in a 17th-century Italianate villa on Cimiez Hill. Boosted by subsequent donations, the collection affords a comprehensive overview of the artist's work, from 1890 through to the gouache cut-outs of his later years. It is made all the more effective by the presentation of items from his daily life (see p44).

2 Promenade des Anglais and Promenade du Paillon

MAP N5–P5, Q4–5

The promenade des Anglais owes its name to the English community that funded its construction in 1822, in order to give work to the local poor. Now flanked by traffic lanes, it sweeps majestically round the Bay of Angels, dotted with belle époque edifices, notably the magnificent Hotel Negresco (see p142). In contrast, the promenade du Paillion cuts a green swathe through the city to the sea and with its central waterway, it provides a tranquil alternative to walking through busy streets. It is also a venue for arts and leisure activities.

The exterior of MAMAC

3 Musée d'Art Moderne et d'Art Contemporain (MAMAC)

MAP Q4 ■ Pl Yves Klein ■ Open 10am–6pm Tue–Sun ■ Closed 1 Jan, Easter, 1 May, 25 Dec ■ Adm

Conceived as a triumphal arch on four marble columns linked by transparent walkways, the museum's modern architecture is startlingly effective. The collections trace the story of the avant garde from the 1960s to the present day. Particularly notable are works by the US Pop Artists and European New Realists, including those by Nice's own Yves Klein (see p40).

4 Vieux Nice

The city's heart, filled with the aroma and sounds of all things Niçoise (see pp20–21).

5 Musée des Beaux-Arts

MAP N5 ■ 33 av des Baumettes ■ Open 10am–6pm Tue–Sun ■ Closed 1 Jan, Easter, 1 May, 25 Dec ■ Adm

The 19th-century town house built for a Ukrainian princess is a marvel of Neo-Classical excess. It holds collections of art from the 17th to early 20th centuries. The first floor provides a panorama of 19th-century French art, through to the Impressionists and Post-Impressionists. On the ground floor are 17th- and 18th-century works, including sculptures by Rodin.

The scenic promenade du Paillon

Opulent interior at Villa Masséna

NICE'S EXPAT COMMUNITY

Led by the British, European (notably Russian) nobility flocked to Nice in wintertime from the early 19th century. Vast, luxurious hotels, villas and places of entertainment sprung up to accommodate them. Nice became two cities – one for the wealthy and leisured northern visitors and another for working Mediterranean natives. This era disappeared with World War I, but somehow the glamour never left.

6 Villa Masséna

MAP Q5 ▪ 65 rue de France ▪ Open 10am–6pm Wed–Mon ▪ Closed 1 Jan, Easter, 1 May, 25 Dec ▪ Adm

This elegant, 19th-century Italianate villa houses the Musée d'Art et d'Histoire, which has an interesting collection covering the period from Bonaparte to the 1930s. Rooms are furnished in First Empire style, and highlights include Napoleon's coronation robe and death mask.

7 Port Lympia

MAP R4

Dug in the 18th century, the port never took off commercially and remains quieter than most Mediterranean city harbours. It is all the more charming for that, a haven of pleasure boats and cruise ships, surrounded by splendid Italianate buildings.

8 Parc Floral Phoenix and Musée des Arts Asiatiques

MAP N5 ▪ 405 promenade des Anglais ▪ Park: open 9:30am–6pm daily (to 7:30pm Apr–Sep, to 7pm early Oct, to 6:30pm late Oct); adm ▪ Museum: open May–mid-Oct: 10am–6pm Wed–Mon; mid-Oct–Apr: 10am–5pm Wed–Mon; closed 1 Jan, 1 May, 25 Dec

This large floral park is a themed wonderland of world horticulture with, at its centre, Europe's biggest greenhouse. Inside the metal and glass "marquee", one wanders through recreated warm-climate zones, from equatorial forest to the Natal desert. Also in the park is the Asian Arts Museum, a marble and glass construction containing classical and contemporary creations from the main Asian civilizations.

Port Lympia

⑨ Cathédrale St-Nicolas
MAP N4 ■ Av Nicolas II
■ Open 9am–noon, 2–6pm Tue–Sun
■ Closed during private religious
events ■ Adm

The Russian community was almost
as prominent in Nice as the British
in the late 19th and early 20th
centuries. This Russian Orthodox
cathedral was completed in 1912
as the community's focal point.

Exterior of the Excelsior Regina Palace

⑩ Cimiez Hill and Musée National Marc Chagall
MAP Q3 ■ Av du Dr Ménard ■ Open
10am–6pm Wed–Mon (to 5pm Nov–
Apr) ■ Closed 1 Jan, 1 May, 25 Dec
■ Adm

When European nobility took to
wintering in Nice, they colonized
Cimiez Hill with magnificent villas in
styles ranging from Louis XV to Neo-
Gothic and Oriental. Most impressive
of all is the Excelsior Regina Palace,
where Queen Victoria once stayed.
Also on Cimiez Hill is the museum
which houses Chagall's 17 great works
on the "Biblical Message" (see p40).
The collection was supplemented
by oil paintings, sketches, pastels
and gouaches, donated by the artist.
Chagall also created stained-glass
windows, a mosaic and tapestry
for the museum.

A MORNING WALK AROUND NICE

▶ Start at the **Tourist Office**
(5 promenade des Anglais), then
turn left along avenue de Verdun
to place Masséna, the city's
central square. Take in the
glorious red façades, gardens
and ornamental fountains before
crossing to enter **Vieux Nice** (see
pp20–21) on rue Alexander Mari.
Turn right into rue de l'Opéra
and left into rue St-François-de-
Paule, an old-fashioned street
with long-established shops,
notably Auer for confectionery
(No. 7) and Alziari for olive oil
(No. 14). Proceed to **cours
Saleya** for the celebrated flower
market, then turn into tiny rue
Gaëtan to soak up the old town
atmosphere. Before leaving the
old town, make sure you take in
the cathedral, the narrow,
Palais Lascaris, place St-François
fish market and the narrow,
shop-filled rue Pairolière.

Emerge into the relative peace
and 18th-century harmony of
place Garibaldi, then take rue
Dr-Ciaudo to the splendid
MAMAC (see p95). You can't miss
the adjacent Bibliothèque Louis
Nucera, designed as a gigantic
human bust with a cube for a
head (2002), before continuing
along **boulevard Carabacel** with
its elaborate mansions.

At **place Magenta**, forget culture
and start shopping. For designer
fashion proceed into rue Paradis
then avenue de Suède. Rue de
Rivoli then brings you to the
legendary **Le Negresco** (see
p143). If you're feeling rich, lunch
in its **Chantecler** restaurant
(see p99); if watching the pennies,
have a look anyway: its interior
abounds in ornate treasures.

See map on p94 ←

Nightspots in Nice

1 Bar des Oiseaux
MAP Q5 ■ Corner of rue St Vincent & rue d'Abbaye ■ Closed Sun, Mon pm

Francophiles will enjoy the theme nights – philosophy, sing-songs and cabaret – while the rest can sip a drink amid a lively crowd at this colourful bar in the old town.

2 La Civette du Cours
MAP Q5 ■ 1 cours Saleya

"Bar sympa", they say in French, which means friendly and appealing – it's especially so for the young, artistic and mildly eccentric.

3 La Cave Romagnan
MAP P4 ■ 22 rue d'Angleterre

One of the oldest wine bars in town, with live music on Saturday nights and local art on the walls.

4 Le Six
MAP Q5 ■ 6 rue Raoul Bosio

In the heart of Vieux Nice, this gay-friendly bar has live music, go-go dancers and karaoke every single night in the summer.

5 Le Relais Piano Bar
MAP N5 ■ 37 promenade des Anglais

No techno here in the bar of the palatial Le Negresco (see p143). Just the tinkling of ivories amid wood panelling and deep armchairs, which give the place the pleasingly languorous air of a gentleman's club.

Le Relais Piano Bar, Le Negresco

Wayne's, a lively British-style pub

6 Wayne's
MAP Q5 ■ 15 rue de la Préfecture

This pub in Vieux Nice is a home-from-home for British expats and tourists. Good beer, pub food, live music, table dancing and a terrace.

7 Ma Nolan's
MAP Q5 ■ 2 rue St-François-de-Paule

This is the number-one Irish pub to go to in Nice. Pints of Guinness, cooked dinners like grandma used to make, televised sport and free Wi-Fi make this a favourite hangout for expats. (One of two locations.)

8 High Club – Studio 47
MAP N5 ■ 45 promenade des Anglais

A popular disco with dancefloors on two levels – the High Club for trendy 20–30-year-olds, and Studio 47 for over-30s in search of a more refined atmosphere.

9 B Spot
MAP P4 ■ 24 av Marechal Foch

This intimate club offers jazz, funk, blues and more, Thursday to Sunday. It is also a popular venue for the Nice Jazz Festival (see p70).

10 La Suite Opera Night Club
MAP Q5 ■ 2 rue Bréa

This top dance club features chic, over-the-top Baroque decor and a range of international DJs.

Places to Eat

PRICE CATEGORIES
For a three-course meal for one with half
a bottle of wine (or equivalent meal),
taxes and extra charges.

€ under €40   €€ €40–€60   €€€ over €60

1 Le Chantecler
MAP N5 ▪ 37 promenade des
Anglais ▪ 04 93 16 64 00 ▪ Closed
Sun, Mon, Tue–Sat L ▪ €€€
Le Chantecler offers a truly palatial
setting within the iconic Le Negresco
for Jean-Denis Rieubland's Michelin-
starred Provençal-inspired haute
cuisine (see p66).

Grand entrance to Le Chantecler

2 Jan
MAP R4 ▪ 12 rue Lascaris
▪ 04 97 19 32 23 ▪ Closed Sun–Mon,
Sat L, Mon L ▪ €€
South African chef Jan Hendrik van
der Westhuizen wows locals and
visitors alike with his twist on the
traditional ingredients of Provence.

3 Chez Acchiardo
MAP Q5 ▪ 38 rue Droite
▪ 04 93 85 51 16 ▪ Closed Sat,
Sun, Aug ▪ No credit cards
▪ No vegetarian dishes ▪ €
Locals sip their apéritifs at the
counter and from the kitchen
comes simple, flavoursome food.

4 Les Viviers
MAP P4 ▪ 22 rue Alphonse
Karr ▪ 04 93 16 00 48 ▪ Closed Sun,
2 weeks Aug ▪ €€
An elegant interior complements
classical seafood dishes and
very impressive desserts.

5 Le Safari
MAP Q5 ▪ 1 cours Saleya
▪ 04 93 80 18 44 ▪ €
Seafood and meat dishes on one of
the liveliest terraces of Vieux Nice.

6 La Merenda
MAP Q5 ▪ 4 rue Raoul Bosio
▪ Closed Sat, Sun, bank hols
▪ No credit cards ▪ €
Dominique le Stanc turned his back
on super-chef stress to open this
little restaurant. Note this reassuringly
simple place has no telephone.

7 Geppetto
MAP Q4 ▪ 5 rue Gioffredo
▪ 04 93 62 47 01 ▪ Closed Sun, Mon–
Thu D ▪ €
Reserve or be prepared to queue for
Nice's most authentic Italian cuisine,
in the city's friendliest dining room.

8 Le Boccacio
MAP Q5 ▪ 7 rue Masséna
▪ 04 93 87 71 76 ▪ €
The decor of this seafood restaurant
recalls that of a schooner – but it's
stylish, rather than kitsch.

9 Alounak
MAP P4 ▪ 3 rue Alsace Lorraine
▪ 04 93 85 86 50 ▪ Closed L, Sun ▪ €
One of the region's top vegetarian
and vegan restaurants (they also
serve meat and seafood dishes).

10 La Petite Loge
MAP Q4 ▪ 10 rue de la Loge
▪ 04 93 01 63 28 ▪ Closed Sun–Wed,
Thu–Sat L ▪ €
Atmospheric wine bar with delicious
tapas-inspired dishes that marry
well with the fabulous array of wines.
It's tiny, so reserve in advance.

See map on p94 ←

TOP 10 Monaco and the Riviera

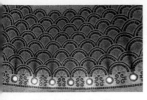

Mosaic domed ceiling, Villa Kerylos

The French Riviera, running from Cannes to the Italian border, is the most mythologized stretch of Mediterranean coastline. In the 19th century its balmy winter climate attracted plutocrats, princes and their entourages, and its clear sunlight and vivid colours drew a new breed of painters. In the 1920s it became a summer resort for the first time, and in the 1950s and 1960s it was the epitome of jet-set chic. In high summer there seems to be hardly a square metre of beach, a yacht mooring, parking space or café table left vacant. Meanwhile, the enclave of Monaco, an independent state since the 14th century, has a character and mystique all of its own.

AREA MAP OF MONACO AND THE RIVIERA

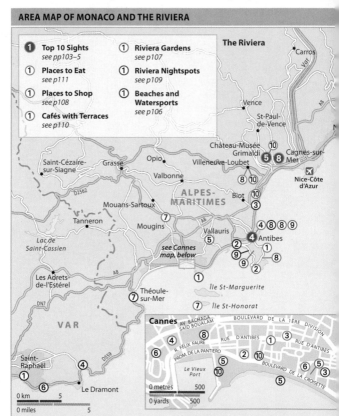

① **Top 10 Sights**
see pp103–5

① **Places to Eat**
see p111

① **Places to Shop**
see p108

① **Cafés with Terraces**
see p110

① **Riviera Gardens**
see p107

① **Riviera Nightspots**
see p109

① **Beaches and Watersports**
see p106

Previous pages Moustiers-Sainte-Marie in the Gorges du Verdon

Interior of Casino de Monte Carlo

1 Casino de Monte Carlo

This monument to *belle époque* splendour is also the heart of the region's famous gambling industry – well worth a look whether you want to play the stakes or simply soak up some glamour *(see pp32–3)*.

2 Villa Ephrussi de Rothschild, St-Jean-Cap-Ferrat

MAP H4 ■ 1 av Ephrussi de Rothschild ■ Open 10am–6pm daily (Jul–Aug: to 7pm); Nov–Feb: 2–6pm Mon–Fri, 10am–6pm Sat–Sun ■ DA to ground floor only ■ Adm

The most palatial of all the villas built in the Riviera's plutocratic heyday was the dream of Beatrice Ephrussi de Rothschild (1864–1934), a daughter of the famous wealthy banking family. Its lavish Neo-Classical façade conceals an opulent interior of arcades surrounded by a covered courtyard hung with magnificent tapestries. Superb antiques and sketches by Fragonard also feature, while the gardens are just as sumptuous as the interior *(see p52)*.

Exterior of the Prince's Palace

3 Prince's Palace, Monaco

MAP H4 ■ Pl du Palais ■ State Rooms and Grands Appartements open: Apr–Oct: 10am–6pm daily ■ Adm

Built on the site of a 13th-century Genoese fortress, the seat of the Grimaldi princes of Monaco is even more imposing inside than out. Highlights include superb frescoes of mythological scenes by 16th-century Genoese artists, the opulent blue-and-gold Louis XV Salon, the finely crafted woodwork of the Mazarin Salon and the gorgeous Throne Room. The cour d'Honneur courtyard, with its geometrical pebble patterns, is a lovely setting for summer concerts. The Compagnie des Carabiniers du Prince, in full dress uniform, changes the guard daily at 11:55am.

4 Musée Picasso, Antibes

MAP G4 ■ Château Grimaldi, Vieux Port ■ Open mid-Jun–mid-Sep: 10am–6pm Tue–Sun (to 8pm Wed & Fri Jul–Aug); mid-Sep–mid-Jun: 10am–noon, 2–6pm Tue–Sun ■ Closed 1 Jan, 1 May, 1 Nov, 25 Dec ■ DA ■ Adm

A bishop's palace in the Dark Ages, this building then fell into the hands of the Grimaldi lords of Monaco, before becoming the seat of the royal governors of the region. Today, it is an art gallery. The museum houses 300 works by Spanish artist Pablo Picasso *(see p40)*, who worked here in 1946 and donated drawings, paintings and over 100 ceramics. Works by other artists, including Miró, Léger, Ernst and Modigliani are also on display *(see p45)*.

Musée Picasso, Antibes

5 Château-Musée Grimaldi, Haut-de-Cagnes

MAP G4 ■ 9 pl Grimaldi ■ Open 10am–noon (Jul & Aug: to 1pm), 2–6pm (Oct–Mar: to 5pm) Wed–Mon ■ Closed 1 Jan, 25 Dec ■ Adm

Built in 1309, this castle's battlements dominate the landscape of Haut-de-Cagnes. Within its walls is a sumptuous palace, built in 1620 by Jean Henri Grimaldi. Today it houses a clutch of museums and art collections including a museum of modern Mediterranean art, a museum dedicated to the olive tree, and a group of portraits of the 1930s *chanteuse*, Suzy Solidor.

View over Roquebrune-Cap-Martin

6 Roquebrune-Cap-Martin

MAP H3 ■ Château de Roquebrune: pl W Ingram, Open 10am–12:30pm, 2–5pm daily (Feb–May: to 6pm); Jun–Sep: 10am–1pm, 2:30–7pm ■ Closed public hols, Fri Nov–Jan ■ Adm ■ www.roquebrune-cap-martin.com

The Château de Roquebrune, perched on its hilltop above Cap-Martin, is said to be the oldest feudal castle in France, built over 1,000 years ago. It has been remodelled often – by the Grimaldi clan and, in the early 20th century, by a wealthy Englishman, Sir William Ingram. At sea level, a lovely coastal path leads all the way to Monaco, passing 19th-century villas in lush gardens *(see p49)*.

7 Musée Oceanographique

MAP H4 ■ Ave St-Martin ■ Open Apr–Jun & Sep: 10am–7pm daily (to 6pm Oct–Nov); Jul–Aug: 9:30am–8pm daily ■ Adm ■ www.oceano.mc

Founded by Prince Albert I in 1910, this clifftop museum features rare species of marine plants and animals, including a shark and coral lagoon.

THE GRIMALDIS OF MONACO

Monaco's Grimaldi dynasty is the oldest ruling family in the world. François Grimaldi, disguised as a monk, seized the castle in 1297. By 1489 France and Savoy recognized Monaco's independence. In 1612 Honore II was the first lord to take the title of prince. During the French Revolution the prince and his family were ousted, to be restored to their throne in 1814.

8 Musée Renoir, Cagnes-sur-Mer

MAP G4 ▪ 19 chemin des Collettes ▪ Open Apr–Sep: 10am–noon, 2–6pm Wed–Mon (10am–1pm Jun–Sep); Oct–Mar: 10am–noon, 2–5pm Wed–Mon ▪ Closed 1 Jan, 1 May, 25 Dec ▪ Adm

The former home of artist Auguste Renoir has been preserved as it was at the time of his death in 1919 (see p45). Eleven of his paintings are on display, including *Les Grandes Baigneuses* (1892), along with some of his sculptures and works by his friends Raoul Dufy and Pierre Bonnard.

9 Salle des Mariages, Menton

MAP H3 ▪ 17 rue de la République ▪ Open 8:30am–noon, 2–4:30pm Mon–Fri ▪ Closed pub hols ▪ Adm

Jean Cocteau decorated this room in Menton's town hall in 1957, adorning it with colourful images of a fishing couple and the story of Orpheus and Eurydice. More of his work can be seen in the Musée Jean Cocteau located on the seafront (see p45).

10 Villa Kerylos, Beaulieu-sur-Mer

MAP H4 ▪ Impasse Gustave Eiffel ▪ Open May & Oct: 10am–6pm daily (Jun–Sep: to 7pm); Nov–Apr: 10am–5pm ▪ DA to ground floor only ▪ Adm ▪ www.villa-kerylos.com

Theodore Reinach (1860–1928) created this stunning building between 1902 and 1908, as a Classical Greek villa, in imitation of the palace of Delos in Greece, dating from the 2nd century BC. Copies of ancient mosaics and frescoes evoke the Greek city states.

Interior of Villa Kerylos

A MORNING TOUR OF THE ROCK

▶ Start this walk around the historical part of Monaco where Europe's oldest ruling family, the Grimaldis founded their principality. Visit the state apartments and the **Prince's Palace** (see p103), taking in the lavish salons, throne room and 17th-century chapel. In one wing is the **Musée des Souvenirs Napoléoniens** (Open Apr–Nov: 10am–6pm daily; Dec–Mar: 10:30am–5pm daily • Adm) housing over 1,000 items, including many of Napoleon Bonaparte's personal effects.

From place du Palais it is a short walk along rue Basse, one of the most picturesque streets in the old quarter, to the **Chapelle de la Visitation**, on place de la Visitation (Open 10am–4pm daily • Adm). Housed in the Baroque chapel are works by artists Rubens and Zurbaran.

At the end of rue Basse, turn right and double back along avenue St-Martin to discover the astonishing sea creatures in the **Musée Oceanographique**). You'll need to allow at least 90 minutes here to view the tanks of marine fauna from all over the world. Don't miss the aquarium with its fearsome sharks. Pause for an early lunch in the museum's restaurant and feast your eyes on the stunning views of the Riviera and the Esterel hills from its terrace before rounding off your visit with the 30-minute ride on the Monaco Tours tourist train. This leaves from the museum on a round trip past the port, the palace, casino and the ornamental gardens.

See map on pp102–3 ←

Beaches and Watersports

1 Vieux Port, St-Raphaël
MAP F5

St-Raphaël is the coast's top dive centre, with shipwrecks from World War II and a range of wall dives off the rocky coast. There are several dive outfits at the Vieux Port – a list is available from the tourist office.

2 Plage Helios, Juan-les-Pins
MAP G4 ■ Open Apr–Sep: 8am–sunset daily ■ Adm ■ DA

A chic private beach, although it does not offer any watersports. As a result, it's perfect for lazing in fashionable luxury on the soft sands.

3 Marineland
A huge family aquapark with 12 chutes, a wave pool and several swimming pools including one for toddlers (see p62).

4 Plage d'Agay
MAP G5

Watersports on this beautiful beach include waterskiing, windsurfing and parascending, as well as more relaxing boat excursions.

5 Plage de la Croisette
MAP G4 ■ Open May–Sep: 8am–sunset daily ■ Adm

One long beach stretches all the way along the Cannes esplanade, sectioned off into tiny private beaches, with parasols, loungers and snack bars with waiter service. Most of the beaches offer waterskiing.

6 Port St-Lucia, St-Raphaël
MAP F5 ■ DA

You can try eight different types of watersports here, including parascending, waterskiing and windsurfing, just outside St-Raphaël.

7 Théoule
MAP G4

The pretty beach at Théoule, surrounded by hills, bustles in summer. Kayaks and pedalos are available to rent.

8 Yacht Club d'Antibes Juan-les-Pins, Antibes
MAP G4 ■ Quai Nord Port Vauban ■ Open 8am–sunset daily

The club offers windsurfing, dinghy and catamaran sailing and yacht charters for all levels, with crewed yachts available by arrangement.

9 Plage Belle-Rives, Juan-les-Pins
MAP G4 ■ 33 bd Edouard Baudoin ■ Open Jun–Sep: 9am–sunset daily ■ Adm ■ DA

This hotel beach offers a great range of adrenaline sports that include bungee-jumping, waterskiing and parascending.

10 Palais des Festivals
MAP G4

Perhaps not the most luxurious beach in Cannes, but it is no more crowded than the pay beaches and it is totally free.

Plage de la Croisette

Riviera Gardens

1 Japanese Garden, Monaco

MAP H4 ■ Av Princesse Grace, Monte Carlo ■ Open 9am–sunset daily ■ DA

This formal garden is a triumph of Zen horticulture and a striking contrast to most of the classic French gardens of the Riviera.

Villa Eilen Roc Gardens

2 Villa Eilen Roc Gardens, Cap d'Antibes

MAP G4 ■ Impasse de Beaumont ■ Open 2–5pm Wed & 1st, 3rd Sat of the month ■ DA ■ Adm Apr–Sep

Charles Garnier, designer of the Monte Carlo Casino, built this villa in a park with trees from all over the world.

3 Jardin Exotique, Monaco

MAP H4 ■ 62 bd du Jardin Exotique ■ Open daily from 9am; Feb–Apr & Oct: to 6pm; May–Sep: to 7pm; Nov–Jan: to 5pm or dusk ■ Closed 19 Nov, 25 Dec ■ Adm ■ www.jardin-exotique.mc

The largest collection of succulent rock plants in the world, plus a 60-m (200-ft) deep cave with spectacular limestone formations (see p53).

4 Casino Gardens, Monaco

MAP H4 ■ Pl du Casino, Monte Carlo ■ Open 9am–sunset daily

Laid out around the casino (see pp32–3) these are classic 19th-century gardens, with trim lawns and water features.

5 Villa Ephrussi de Rothschild

Gorgeous formal gardens and lily ponds surround the pink-and-white villa built by Beatrice Ephrussi de Rothschild (see p103).

6 Parc Fontvieille and Princess Grace Rose Garden, Monaco

MAP H4 ■ Fontvieille ■ Open sunrise–sunset daily ■ DA

Here are palm and olive groves, plus a lake surrounded by 4,000 roses planted in memory of Princess Grace of Monaco.

7 Jardin Exotique, Èze

MAP H4 ■ Rue du Château ■ Open daily from 9am; Apr, May & Jun: to 6:30pm; Jul–Sep: to 7:30pm; Oct–Mar: to 4:30pm; Nov & Dec: to 4:30pm ■ Adm

The exotic gardens around the cliff-top village offer superb sea views.

8 Jardin Botanique Exotique, Menton

MAP H3 ■ Av St-Jacques ■ Open Wed–Mon; May–Aug: 10am–12:30pm, 3:30–6:30pm; Sep-Apr: 10am–12:30pm, 2–5pm ■ Closed 1 May ■ Adm

Laid out by Lord Radcliffe in 1905, this garden is planted with a wide range of subtropical shrubs.

9 Parc Thuret, Cap d'Antibes

MAP G4 ■ 62 bd du Cap ■ Open Mon–Fri; summer: 8am–6pm; winter: 8:30am–5:30pm ■ Closed pub hols ■ DA

Superb collection of trees and shrubs founded by Gustave Thuret in 1857.

10 Parc de Vaugrenier, Villeneuve-Loubet

MAP G4 ■ Bd des Groules, RN7 dir Villeneuve-Loubet ■ Open 24 hours daily ■ DA

Numerous rare plants can be seen in this park, which also features walking trails and a freshwater lagoon.

See map on pp102–3

Places to Shop

1 Rue d'Antibes, Cannes
MAP G4

For that absolutely fabulous Cannes look, head straight for rue d'Antibes and its string of designer boutiques, all breathtakingly expensive and dazzlingly ostentatious.

2 Avenue des Beaux-Arts and Allée Serge Diaghilev, Monaco
MAP H4

With plenty of cash floating around, Monaco is a magnet for designer shops and haute couture. Try these two streets for the latest look.

3 La Croisette, Cannes
MAP G4

Cannes' famous esplanade is a great place for shopping or window-shopping, with famous labels such as Chanel (at No. 5), Christian Dior (No. 38), Celine (No. 43), Louis Vuitton (No. 22) and Cartier (No. 57).

Produce on sale at Le Marché Forville

4 Le Marché Forville, Cannes
MAP G4

This open-air market overflows with flowers, seasonal fruit and vegetables, fresh fish and local products. It's a great place to buy Provençal delicacies to take home. Open daily except Mondays, when it becomes a flea market.

5 Vallauris
MAP H4

Vallauris's moribund pottery industry was revived when Picasso took an interest in the craft, and more than 100 local potters sell their work on its streets in summer.

6 Galerie du Metropole, Monaco
MAP H4

Get the Monaco look at an affordable price at this shopping centre which houses a selection of designer shops selling prêt-à-porter clothes, shoes and accessories.

7 Nouvelles Galeries, Menton
MAP H3 ■ Rue de la République

You will find four levels of international designer and brand-name clothes and accessories for men, women and children, all under one roof. There is free parking, too.

8 Cours Masséna, Antibes
MAP G4

One of the last authentic covered markets on the Riviera bustles with life every morning until noon. It is the perfect place for buying all sorts of local delicacies to take home.

9 Antiques Market, Antibes
MAP G4 ■ Pl Audiberti, pl de la Liberté, bd d'Aguillon, pl Nationale

Rummage through stalls – selling everything from cut glass and statuary to antique porcelain, lace, embroidery and linen – in search of something small enough to carry home. Thursday and Saturdays, from 8am to noon.

10 Villeneuve-Loubet
MAP G4

Villeneuve-Loubet supports a thriving arts scene and is full of artists' and sculptors' studios where you can invest in an original work of art by a living artist.

Riviera Nightspots

1 Le Baoli, Cannes
MAP G4 ■ La Croisette
■ Open from 8pm Fri–Sat (nightly
Apr–Oct and during festivals) ■ DA
■ www.lebaoli.com

One of the Riviera's best venues,
this cool but expensive club-
restaurant attracts the likes of Bono
and Naomi Campbell to its Asian-
style garden of delights.

2 Casino de Monte Carlo
This is the epitome of Riviera
glamour, luxury and gambling
excess *(see pp32–3)*.

Salle Europe, Casino de Monte Carlo

3 Carlton Bar, Cannes
MAP G4 ■ Carlton
InterContinental Cannes, 58 La
Croisette

It is billed as "the place to have a
drink in the company of stars", but
even during the Film Festival you
are unlikely to rub shoulders with
the A list. Nonetheless, it is one of
the best bars in Cannes.

4 Jimmy'z, Monaco
MAP H4 ■ Le Sporting Club, av
Princess Grace ■ 00 377 98 06 70 68
■ Open 11:30pm–dawn daily

Opened in 1974, Jimmy'z is still *the*
place to party in Monaco, attracting
the rich, famous and beautiful, and
hosting top-name DJs. Of course all
this glamour comes at a steep price.
Make sure you dress to impress.

**5 Casino Barrière Le
Croisette, Cannes**
MAP G4 ■ 1 Jetée Albert Édouard/
1 Espace Lucien Barrière ■ Open daily
to 5am in summer ■ DA ■ www.
lucienbarriere.com

Within walking distance of the Palais
des Festivals and overlooking the
busy Croisette, this casino offers one
of the city's largest and most elegant
gaming rooms.

6 Charly's Bar, Cannes
MAP G4 ■ 5 rue Suquet
■ 04 97 06 54 78

With its stone-walled, cave-like
interior, open-door policy, and DJs
and dancing every night, the party
crowd keeps coming back to this
old favourite.

7 Blue Gin, Monaco
MAP H4 ■ The Monte Carlo
Bay Hotel, 40 ave Princess Grace
■ 377 98 06 06 77 ■ DA

As the name suggests gin is the drink
of choice here, with 17 different
varieties on offer. Most guests,
however, come to sit on the terrace
and admire the beautiful sea view.

8 Disco 7, Cannes
MAP G4 ■ 7 rue Rouguière

Loud and louche, Disco 7 (or Le 7
Cabaret) attracts a mixed gay
and straight crowd. Techno and
transvestism make for a wonderfully
flamboyant atmosphere.

9 Stars 'N' Bars, Monaco
MAP H4 ■ 6 quai Antoine 1
■ www.starsnbars.com

One of the most popular club-
restaurants in Monaco, the
transatlantic music and menu
attracts a young, wealthy clientele.

10 B.Pub, Cannes
MAP G4 ■ 22 rue Macé

Open every night with DJs or live
music, this club is frequented by the
cool crowd. Don't miss the moment
when the bar bursts into flames.

See map on pp102–3 ←

Cafés with Terraces

1 Café de Paris, Monte Carlo
MAP H4 ■ Pl du Casino

In front of the casino (see p33), under white umbrellas and baskets of flowers with the Mediterranean in the background, the Café de Paris is a delightful place for an al fresco meal or a drink.

2 Le Majestic Barrière, Cannes
MAP G4 ■ 10 La Croisette

Sip your drinks slowly on this deeply fashionable hotel terrace that attracts the crème de la crème of the film business during the International Film Festival. It's very pricey – a glass of bubbly here costs as much as a meal in many other spots.

3 La Trattoria, Monte Carlo
MAP H4 ■ Le Sporting d'été, av Princesse Grace ■ Open dinner only

Famed chef Alain Ducasse's terrace restaurant serves gourmet antipasti, pizzas and gelati in summer. After dinner, skip the queue to get into Jimmy'z next door (see p109) via the private entrance.

4 Chèvre d'Or, Èze
It's worth staying at this gorgeous château hotel just to enjoy breakfast on its clifftop terrace, with breathtaking views out over the sea below (see p144).

5 Carlton Terrace, Cannes
MAP G4 ■ Carlton InterContinental Cannes, 58 La Croisette

The terrace of the Carlton InterContinental is the top place to see and be seen in Cannes, with a superior view of the bay and promenaders along the Croisette.

6 Villa Ephrussi de Rothschild, St-Jean-Cap-Ferrat
The villa's delightful tea room and terrace, overlooking beautiful gardens and with panoramic views of the bay of Villefranche, is one of the most magical and idyllic places for a light lunch or tea along the entire Riviera (see p103).

7 Bar du Mas, Mougins
MAP G4 ■ Le Mas Candille, bd Clément Rebuffel

Admire the Grasse countryside as you sip a chilled glass of rosé on the stone terrace of this luxury hotel. It's a much more affordable option than staying here.

8 Plage de la Garoupe, Cap d'Antibes
MAP G4 ■ Closed Sun pm

Walk along the eastern shore of this exclusive part of the Riviera, and you'll come to a short strip of private beaches with several cafés.

9 Mirazur, Menton
MAP H3 ■ 30 av Aristide Briand

The most breathtaking views over Menton and its port are from the lofty garden terrace of the chic restaurant Mirazur, next to the oldest avocado tree in France.

10 Le Cactus, Èze
MAP H4 ■ 3 rue Brec

If your budget won't stretch to the Chèvre d'Or, this modest café has the same stunning views for a fraction of the price and serves delicious crêpes.

Chèvre d'Or terrace, Èze

Places to Eat

PRICE CATEGORIES
For a three-course meal for one with half a bottle of wine (or equivalent meal), taxes and extra charges.

€ under €40 €€ €40–€60 €€€ over €60

Terrace of Bacon at Cap d'Antibes

1 Bacon, Cap d'Antibes
MAP G4 ▪ 668 bd de Bacon ▪ 04 93 61 50 02 ▪ Closed Mon, Tue L, Nov–Feb ▪ DA ▪ €€€

This legendary fish restaurant has fine views over the Baie des Anges.

2 La Table du Royal, St-Jean-Cap-Ferrat
MAP H4 ▪ 3 av Jean Monnet ▪ 04 93 76 31 00 ▪ Closed mid-Nov–mid-Jan & mid-Aug–Sep ▪ DA ▪ €€€

La Table du Royal offers elegant, modern cuisine and Riviera views.

3 La Cave, Cannes
MAP G4 ▪ 9 bd de la République ▪ 04 93 99 79 87 ▪ Closed Mon & Sat L, Sun ▪ €€

La Cave has built its stellar reputation for excellent food since 1989.

4 Le Vauban, Antibes
MAP G4 ▪ 7 rue Thuret ▪ 04 93 34 33 05 ▪ Closed Tue, Mon & Wed L, 1 week June ▪ €€

Le Vauban offers perfect renditions of French and Provençal classics.

5 Pulcinella, Monte Carlo
MAP H4 ▪ 17 rue du Portier ▪ 00 377 93 30 73 61 ▪ DA ▪ €€

Delicious Italian food is the speciality in this lovely restaurant. Photos of celebrity regulars line the walls.

6 3.14 Resto, Cannes
MAP G4 ▪ Hotel 3.14, 5 rue François-Einesy ▪ 04 92 99 72 00 ▪ Closed L, Sun, Mon ▪ DA ▪ €€

Purple velvet and chandeliers set the tone in the only organic and gluten-free restaurant in Cannes.

7 La Tonnelle, Île St-Honorat
MAP G4 ▪ 04 92 99 54 08 ▪ Closed D, mid-Nov–mid-Dec ▪ DA ▪ €€

This restaurant offers splendid views and a fish-based lunch. Wines are made by the resident monks.

8 L'Auberge Fleurie, Villeneuve-Loubet
MAP G4 ▪ Rue des Mesures ▪ 04 93 73 90 92 ▪ Closed Mon, Sun D, Tue–Thu ▪ DA ▪ €€

Eat delicious Peach Melba just steps from the birthplace of the dish's creator, Escoffier.

The terrace at Les Deux Frères

9 Les Deux Frères, Roquebrune, Cap Martin
MAP H4 ▪ Pl des Deux Frères ▪ 04 93 28 99 00 ▪ Closed Sun D, Mon, Tue L, mid-Oct–mid-Nov ▪ €€€

Provençale dishes based on lamb, duck and seafood are served in this delightful restaurant.

10 Le Pérousin, Cagnes-sur-Mer
MAP G4 ▪ 4 rue Hippolyte Guis ▪ 09 53 55 61 92 ▪ Closed Wed, Nov ▪ €

The intimate setting is as charming as the seasonal cuisine, which includes dishes cooked on an open fire.

See map on pp102–3 ←

🔟 Alpes-Maritimes

Technically, the Riviera is part of the Alpes-Maritimes *département*, but inland the landscape changes dramatically and the region's forested mountains, deep river gorges and medieval hilltop villages seem a million miles from the busy seaside resorts. High in the mountains is the Mercantour, a region of rocky summits and glaciers, which shelters chamois, ibex and rare lammergeier vultures. In winter, Alpes-Maritimes is one of France's favourite ski areas.

La Trophée des Alpes at La Turbie

1 La Trophée des Alpes

MAP H3 ▪ Cours Albert 1er, La Turbie ▪ Open Tue–Sun; mid-Sep–mid-May: 10am–1:30pm, 2:30–5pm; mid-May–mid-Sep: 9:30am–1pm, 2:30–6:30pm ▪ Closed public hols ▪ Adm

This remarkable Roman monument is the only one of its kind still in existence. It can be seen from afar and offers fine views along the Riviera. A museum shows a 3-D film about the monument's history (see p42).

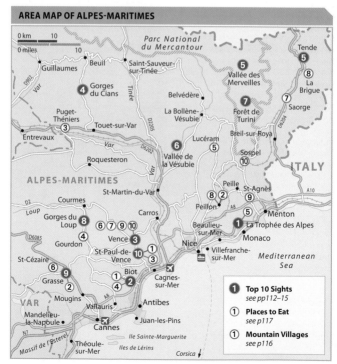

AREA MAP OF ALPES-MARITIMES

🔟	**Top 10 Sights** see pp112–15
①	**Places to Eat** see p117
①	**Mountain Villages** see p116

The medieval village of Vence, perched atop a crag

2 Biot

MAP G4 ■ Musée Fernand Léger: Chemin du Val-de-Pôme; open 10am–5pm Wed–Mon (to 6pm May–Oct); closed 1 Jan, 1 May, 25 Dec; adm; http://musees-nationaux-alpesmaritimes.fr/fleger ■ La Verrerie de Biot: Chemin des Combes; open 9:30am–7:30pm Mon–Sat (to 6pm in winter), 10:30am–1:30pm, 2:30–7:30pm Sun & pub hols (to 6pm in winter); adm; www.verreriebiot.com ■ www.biot.fr

The pretty little town of Biot sits on a hilltop among pinewoods. It is renowned for its high-quality decorative glassware, which you can watch being blown at La Verrerie de Biot. The wonderful Musée Fernand Léger, also in the village, contains more than 400 drawings and paintings by the artist *(see p44)*.

3 Vence

MAP G4

Vence is a gem of the region, with an unbeatable location on a high crag, and sweeping views. The medieval centre is ringed by formidable battlement walls and is entered through a massive stone gateway, to a labyrinth of cobbled streets and tall stone houses. A small cathedral, dating from the 11th century and built on the site of a Roman temple, stands on place Clemenceau.

4 Gorges du Cians

MAP G3

The deep gorge carved through the mountains by the River Cians is made all the more spectacular by the deep red of the exposed rock. The river descends 1,600 m (5,250 ft) in just 25 km (15 miles) between the hilltop villages of Beuil and Touet-sur-Var, where the Cians meets the larger river Var. The canyon is at its narrowest and most spectacular at Pra d'Astier, which is about midway between the two villages *(see p50)*.

Gorges du Cians

5 Vallée des Merveilles and Musée des Merveilles

MAP H2 ■ Musée des Merveilles: av du 16 Septembre 1947, Tende; open 10am–6pm Wed–Mon (to 5pm mid-Sep–mid-Jun; daily Jul–Sep); closed 1 Jan, 2 wks mid-Mar, 1 May, 2 wks mid-Nov, 25 Dec; DA

High in the Parc National du Mercantour *(see p50)*, this valley shelters a treasury of Bronze Age art *(see p36)*. Rock carvings dating from 1800–1500 BC are scattered over the slopes of the 2,870-m (9,400-ft) Mont Bégo. They are almost impossible to find without a guide, but the Musée des Merveilles has many examples.

Petroglyphs, Vallée des Merveilles

6 Vallée de la Vésubie

MAP H3 ■ www.vesubian.com

Two streams merge at St-Martin-Vésubie to form the River Vésubie, which flows through landscapes of pinewoods, meadows, forested peaks and narrow canyons to join the Var 24 km (15 miles) north of Nice. The valley is dotted with attractive

Pointe des Trois Communes

SKIING IN THE ALPES D'AZUR

High above the balmy coast, the slopes and summits of the Alpes d'Azur **(above)** are deeply covered in snow in winter, with excellent skiing conditions, and there are more than 250 pistes, ranging from black to green runs, in well-equipped resorts. The best known is Isola 2000, with 5 black runs, 14 red, 13 blue and 4 green.

villages, and the river is at its most scenic where it passes through the Gorges de la Vésubie, a canyon of coloured rock walls.

7 Forêt de Turini

MAP H3

A moist micro-climate, created by warm sea air rising over the cooler mountains, waters this mountain forest, where thick beech, maple and chestnut woods cloak the lower slopes and huge pines rise on the higher mountainsides. From Pointe des Trois Communes, on the fringe of the forest at an altitude of 2,082 m (6,830 ft), there is a panorama of the Alpine foothills and the Parc National du Mercantour *(see p50)*.

8 Gorges du Loup
MAP G3

The most spectacular of the region's river canyons, the River Loup has sliced its way deep into the rock to create a series of waterfalls. These include the 40-m (130-ft) Cascade de Courmes, rapids and deep potholes, such as the Saut du Loup (see p51).

9 Grasse
MAP G4 ■ Musée Internationale de la Parfumerie: 2 bd du Jeu du Ballon; open Apr–Sep: 10am–7pm daily; Oct–Mar 10:30am–5:30pm Wed–Mon; closed 1 Jan, 1 May, 25 Dec; adm

Grasse is a rather dull town at first sight, but its air is scented by the perfume factories for which it has been famous for over four centuries. Vast quantities of blooms are processed here for their essential oils, and a spectacular jasmine festival is held each August.
You can buy perfumes at the Musée Internationale de la Parfumerie.

The diminutive Fondation Maeght

10 Fondation Maeght, St-Paul-de-Vence
MAP G4 ■ Montée des Trious ■ Open 10am–6pm daily (Jul–Sep: to 7pm) ■ Adm

One of the finest small modern art museums in the world, the Maeght includes work by Marc Chagall, Joan Miró, Fernand Léger, Alexander Calder, Alberto Giacometti, and many more 20th-century artists. Works are exhibited in rotation; the only works on permanent display are the large sculptures in the grounds (see p44).

A WALK THROUGH MEDIEVAL VENCE

A giant ash tree, Le Frêne (The Ash) is your landmark for the beginning of this two-hour stroll through the old quarter of **Vence** (see p113), with its stone-paved streets and medieval houses, which huddle inside a ring of 13th-century battlements. Before entering the walls through the 16th-century Porte de Peyra, visit the **Château de Villeneuve**, which hosts a changing programme of modern art and design exhibitions.

After walking through the gateway, turn right, and allow half an hour to walk along the **rue du Marché**, where the rows of shops selling herbs, fruit, fresh pasta and fish will make your mouth water. At the end of the rue du Marché, turn left and walk across **place Surian** and **place Clemenceau** to the **Cathédrale Notre Dame de la Nativité** – look out for Roman inscriptions dating back almost 2,000 years on the masonry of the buildings either side of it, carved when Vence was the Roman settlement of Vintium. Also look for the oak choir stalls carved with satirical figures, commissioned by a witty 17th-century bishop.

Leave the square by its north side, through the arched **passage Cahors**, then walk up **rue du Seminaire** and turn left to follow the old quarter along **rue de la Coste**. Leave the old quarter by the **Portail Levis**, which takes you back on to place du Frêne. There are several cafés and restaurants here, such as **Auberge des Seigneurs** (see p117) where you can enjoy a drink and snack.

See map on p112 ←

Mountain Villages

1 St-Paul-de-Vence

MAP G4

The prettiest and best known of the region's *villages perchés (see p88)*, St-Paul was first built as a refuge from Saracen raiders. From its ramparts there are terrific views down to the sea *(see p48)*.

Beautiful St-Paul-de-Vence

2 Peillon

MAP H3

Peillon's red-tiled houses seem to grow out of the hilltop itself, rising in tiers to a cobbled square with great views of the forested valley. It seems barely changed since the Middle Ages.

3 Puget-Théniers
MAP G3

The village of Puget-Théniers stands where the Roudoule river meets the Var, overlooked by the ruins of the Château-Musée Grimaldi *(see p104)*. The 13th-century Knights Templar church has a beautiful 16th-century altarpiece *(see p47)*.

4 Gourdon
MAP G4

From the village square, where the hillside drops into a limestone gorge, you can see all the way down the Loup valley to the coast.

5 Lucéram
MAP H3

Here, tall old houses are set around a 17th-century Rococo church and an onion-domed clock tower.

6 St-Cézaire-sur-Siagne

MAP F4 ■ Grottes de St-Cézaire: rte de Grasse; open 10am–noon, 2–5pm (Jun-Aug: to 6pm); closed mid-Nov–Jan; adm

This hill village has been inhabited since the Roman era and has medieval walls and watch towers. Nearby are the grottoes of St-Cézaire, an underground wonderland.

7 Saorge

MAP H3

The clifftop location rivals Gourdon's for dizzying effect, and the village is a little-changed crescent of 15th- to 17th-century pastel houses. It has two pretty churches, and splendid views.

8 La Brigue

MAP H2

Unspoilt La Brigue has cobbled streets, arcaded buildings and the church of Notre-Dame-des-Fontaines, with its superb medieval frescoes.

9 St-Agnès
MAP H3

At 671 m (2,200 ft), St-Agnès is the highest of the coastal *villages perchés*. There are some great walking trails nearby, in the Gorbio valley.

10 Sospel
MAP H3

Colourful arcaded houses and a Baroque church are features of this pretty mountain village near the Italian border. Badly damaged in World War II, it has now been lovingly restored.

Colourful houses in Sospel

Places to Eat

PRICE CATEGORIES

For a three-course meal for one with half a bottle of wine (or equivalent meal), taxes and extra charges.

€ under €40 ■ €€ €40–€60 ■ €€€ over €60

1 Les Terraillers, Biot

MAP G4 ■ 11 rte Chemin Neuf ■ 04 93 65 01 59 ■ Closed Wed, Thu, mid-Oct–Nov ■ €€€

This sophisticated restaurant is set in a 16th-century pottery mill. The dishes are rich and flavourful and the wine list superb.

2 Bastide St-Antoine, Grasse

MAP G4 ■ 48 av Henri Dunant ■ 04 93 70 94 94 ■ Closed last week Feb ■ DA ■ €€€

This restaurant serves gastronomic dishes such as roast monkfish with Kristal caviar and a fennel confit flavoured with star anise.

3 Le St-Paul, St-Paul-de-Vence

MAP G4 ■ 86 rue Grande ■ 04 93 32 65 25 ■ Closed Nov–Mar ■ €€€

Part of a stunning hideaway hotel, Le St-Paul serves fine seafood and other dishes in a stylish dining room or on a terrace with great views from the village battlements.

4 Le Jarrier, Biot

MAP G4 ■ 30 passage de la Bourgade ■ 04 92 95 97 79 ■ Closed Thu ■ €€

Hidden away in a side street, this restaurant offers fantastic value for money, a pretty terrace and live music at weekends.

5 Hostellerie Jerome, La Turbie

MAP H3 ■ 20 rue Comte de Cessole ■ 04 92 41 51 51 ■ Closed L, Dec–mid-Feb ■ €€€

Only open in the evenings, this fine restaurant serves inventive dishes such as scampi in a *verveine* crust.

6 Auberge des Seigneurs, Vence

MAP G4 ■ 1 rue Dr Binet ■ 04 93 58 04 24 ■ Closed Sun, Mon, mid-Dec–mid-Jan ■ No vegetarian options ■ DA ■ €

Renowned spit-roasted local lamb and chicken are among the mouth-watering choices at this friendly medieval inn on the edge of the old quarter, complete with an open fire.

7 Les Bacchanales, Vence

MAP G4 ■ 247 av de Provence ■ 04 93 24 19 19 ■ Closed Tue, Wed, two weeks mid-Dec ■ DA ■ €€€

Chef Christophe Dufau uses simple, local ingredients to create inventive, masterful modern European cuisine.

Dish at Les Bacchanales

8 Auberge de la Madone, Peillon

MAP H3 ■ 3 pl Auguste Arnulf ■ 04 93 07 91 17 ■ Closed Wed, mid-Nov–Jan ■ €€€

Enjoy classic Provençal cuisine on a terrace overlooking a medieval village.

9 Les Lavandes, Vence

MAP G4 ■ Rue du Marché ■ 04 93 32 61 52 ■ Closed Mon & Thu L, Wed ■ €€

The husband-and-wife team here serve delicious Franco-Thai cuisine.

10 La Farigoule, Vence

MAP G4 ■ 15 av Henri-Isnard ■ 04 93 58 01 27 ■ Closed Mon, Tue, late Nov–Christmas ■ €

Two sensibly priced menus offer mouthwatering classical cuisine.

See map on p112

🔟 Alpes-de-Haute-Provence

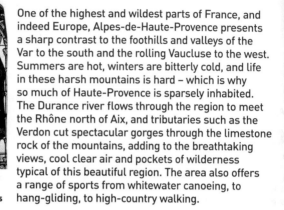

One of the highest and wildest parts of France, and indeed Europe, Alpes-de-Haute-Provence presents a sharp contrast to the foothills and valleys of the Var to the south and the rolling Vaucluse to the west. Summers are hot, winters are bitterly cold, and life in these harsh mountains is hard – which is why so much of Haute-Provence is sparsely inhabited. The Durance river flows through the region to meet the Rhône north of Aix, and tributaries such as the Verdon cut spectacular gorges through the limestone rock of the mountains, adding to the breathtaking views, cool clear air and pockets of wilderness typical of this beautiful region. The area also offers a range of sports from whitewater canoeing, to hang-gliding, to high-country walking.

Stained glass at Moustiers

AREA MAP OF ALPES-DE-HAUTE-PROVENCE

1 **Top 10 Sights**
see pp119–21

1 **Places to Eat**
see p123

1 **Towns and Villages**
see p122

Aerial view over Moustiers-Sainte-Marie

as the 9th century AD, when it was ruled by the bishops of Sisteron and the princes of Lurs. Deserted in the 19th century, it has now become an artists' colony. There are stupendous views from the Promenade des Evêques (Bishops' Walk) leading to the chapel of Notre-Dame-de-Vie, especially colourful in spring when the wildflowers bloom.

1 Moustiers-Sainte-Marie
MAP E3 ▪ Musée de la Faïence: rue Bourgade; open mid-Mar–Oct: 10am–12:30pm, 2–6pm Wed–Mon (Jul & Aug: to 7pm); Nov & Dec: 10am–12.30pm, 2–5pm Sat, Sun & school hols; adm (free Tue)

Moustiers, loud with the sound of a swift-running stream which flows through the middle of the village, is simply delightful, with its tall old houses, plane trees and, for those who can face the climb, a superb view of the Gorges du Verdon from the clifftop church of Notre-Dame-de-Beauvoir (see p48). The village is famed for its faïence ware, and you can see wonderful examples in the Musée de la Faïence (see p48).

2 Mont Pelat
MAP F2

The highest peak in the Provençal Alps rises to a height of 3,050 m (10,020 ft) and dominates a lofty landscape of bare rocky summits, marked by snow until early summer, pine forests and alpine meadows. The massif is crossed by breathtaking passes, including the Cime de la Bonette, by which the D64 road traverses the shoulder of Mont Pelat at a dizzy height of 2,860 m (9,400 ft), making it the highest pass in Europe.

3 Lurs
MAP D3

Founded before the reign of Charlemagne, during the Dark Ages, the town of Lurs was fortified as early

4 Montagne de Lure
MAP D2

Deep in the heart of the Luberon, the Lure mountain – an extension of the savage massif of Mont Ventoux in neighbouring Vaucluse (see p125) – is Provence at its wildest, least hospitable and, some would say, its loveliest. Abandoned hamlets are reminders of Provence in the first half of the 20th century, when many rural people gave up trying to scrape a living from this harsh countryside.

5 Ville Forte, Entrevaux
MAP F3

The citadel of Entrevaux is one of the most dramatic of all the region's many fortresses. Perched on a pinnacle above this fairytale town, it can be reached only by a steep, zigzag path which passes through more than a dozen arched gateways. Lying beneath it, the impregnable Ville Forte is ringed by towers and ramparts and reached by a drawbridge over the river Var.

A tower in Ville Forte, Entrevaux

Citadelle de Sisteron, over the Durance

6 Citadelle de Sisteron

MAP E2 ■ Pl de la Citadelle
■ Open Apr–Nov: from 9am daily
(Apr: to 6pm; May: to 6:30pm; Jun &
Sep: to 7pm; Jul & Aug: to 7:30pm;
Oct: to 5:30pm; Nov: 10am–5pm);
other times by appt only (call 04 92
61 27 57) ■ Adm

Squatting on a steep-sided crag,
high above the narrow valley of the
River Durance, the formidable
defences of the Citadelle guard one
of the strategic gateways to Provence
(see p48). Built in the 13th century,
the bastions and ramparts, crowned
by towers and a chapel, are a great
piece of military engineering. In the
summer, they become the venue for
the Nuits de la Citadelle, a festival of
music, theatre and dance.

7 Fort de Savoie, Colmars-les-Alpes

MAP F2 ■ 04 92 74 09 59 ■ Open Jul–
Aug: 2:30–7pm daily by appt ■ Adm

Perched atop medieval walls, this
17th-century fortress has a grim,

Fort de Savoie, Colmars-les-Alpes

NAPOLEON AT SISTERON

On 1 March 1815 Napoleon Bonaparte
escaped from exile on Elba and landed
at Golfe Juan. Had the citadel at
Sisteron been garrisoned by Royalist
troops, his attempt to regain his
Imperial throne might have been
foiled, but he entered the town
unopposed on 5 March to begin
a triumphal progress to Paris, only
to meet his final defeat at Waterloo.

businesslike look when compared
with the fairytale medieval castles
found elsewhere in Provence. It was
built to withstand cannon fire, not just
arrows and siege towers. The work
of master military engineer Vauban,
it is a testimony to his skill. The Fort
de France, the second of this former
frontier garrison's strongholds, has
fared less well and lies in ruins.

8 Forcalquier

MAP D3 ■ Couvent des
Cordeliers: bd des Martyrs; open
10am–1pm, 3–6:30pm Mon–Sat;
adm ■ www.forcalquier.com

This beguiling old town was once
the seat of powerful local lords
and the capital of the region. One
gate of the old walled town, the Porte
des Cordeliers, still survives, along
with the restored cloisters and stark
library of the 13th-century Couvent
des Cordeliers, with its tombs of
the town's medieval *seigneurs*. The
convent is home to Les Hommes de
la Lavande, which celebrates all
aspects of lavender cultivation.

9 Parc Naturel Régional du Verdon

MAP E3, F3

Along the river Verdon, this regional park is a huge patchwork of landscapes, ranging from the neatly cultivated lavender fields of the sunlit Valensole plateau to the forested hills and pastures of the Artuby, the awesome chasms of the Gorges du Verdon (see pp14–15) and the beginnings of the Alps. There are brilliant blue lakes created where the Verdon has been dammed. This is a paradise for hikers, with a network of 700 km (450 miles) of paths, bridleways and ancient mule highways.

Lavender fields of the Valensole plateau

10 Musée de la Préhistoire des Gorges du Verdon

MAP E3 ■ Rte de Montmeyan, 04500 Quinson ■ 04 92 74 09 59 for cave tours ■ Museum: open Feb–Mar & Oct–mid-Dec: 10am–6pm Wed– Mon (to 7pm Apr–Jun, Sep); Jul, Aug: 10am–8pm daily; closed mid-Dec–Jan; adm

This museum, in a building designed by British architect Norman Foster, traces the geological, cultural and environmental evolution of human life in the Verdon and throughout Europe, with a fascinating series of displays and interactive exhibits. Guided tours visit caves where relics of early humans have been found.

A MORNING DRIVE THROUGH THE CANYON

Start after breakfast from the unassuming little market town of **Castellane** (see p122), gateway to the canyons, and drive west on D952. The landscape becomes progressively more awe-inspiring as you enter the gorges and wind your way through towering walls of rock to **Point Sublime** (see p14). This is one of the most impressive viewpoints on the tour; savour it while enjoying a coffee or a cold drink at the pleasant **Auberge du Point Sublime** (see p123).

From here, drive for about 15 minutes and turn left on to the vertiginous route des Crêtes, which winds past a series of ever higher viewpoints. Don't rush this part of the drive, but stop at each one for five or ten minutes, as the views vary all the time and each one is special. Finally, the road swings around the shoulder of the massif, and far below you is the Verdon and the plateau country around the little village of **La Palud sur Verdon** (see p122). It will take you another 30 minutes to get there, so relax when you do with another coffee at one of the village restaurants.

When you are ready to set off again from La Palud, you'll find it a less daunting drive until the gorgeous turquoise waters of the **Lac de Ste-Croix** (see p15) come into sight. The road runs high above the lake, bringing you to the delightfully pretty village of **Moustiers-Ste-Marie**. Reward yourself with lunch here, since the village happens to have two of the region's best restaurants, La Treille Muscate and Ferme Ste-Cécile (see p123).

See map on p118 ←

Towns and Villages

The beautiful mountain town of Seyne-les-Alpes

1 Seyne-les-Alpes
MAP E2

Military and religious buildings are scattered through this quiet mountain town: a 15th-century gate, a medieval church and a ruined citadel are the main points of interest.

2 Les Mées
MAP E3

The little village of Les Mées is known for the strange rock formations called the Pénitents des Mées. Legend says these pinnacles were monks who broke their vows of chastity and were turned to stone by St Donat *(see p39)*.

3 Simiane-la-Rotonde
MAP D3

The enigmatic Rotonde, a Roman relic, whose purpose is still a puzzle, crowns the village to which it lends its name, a picturesque cluster of old houses and churches, as well as a ramshackle medieval fort.

4 Annot
MAP F3

Annot stands in unspoilt countryside in the Vaire valley. Many houses are built into the giant sandstone glacial boulders, known as the *grès d'Annot* – some have 17th- and 18th-century carved façades.

5 La Palud sur Verdon
MAP E3

La Palud stands on the north side of the Gorges du Verdon, making it a very popular base for exploring the region *(see pp14–15)*.

6 Castellane
MAP F3

Castellane is a lively market town surrounded by steep mountains. The Verdon flows through it, and it is a centre for adventure sports *(see p15)*.

7 Allemagne en Provence
MAP E3

Allemagne en Provence lies between the rugged canyon country of the Verdon and the lavender fields of the Valensole plateau. It is dominated by the splendidly palatial 12th-century Château d'Allemagne.

8 St-André-les-Alpes
MAP F3

This little village bustles in summer. Built where the Verdon and Issole rivers flow into the man-made Lac de Castillon, it is a popular watersports centre, with dinghies, windsurfers and canoes for hire.

9 Beauvezer
MAP F2

Beauvezer, in the dramatic Vallée du Haut Verdon, stands 1,179 m (3,600 ft) above sea level. It enjoys a pristine natural setting, near two major ski resorts (Le Seignus and La Foux).

10 Barcelonnette
MAP F2

Provence's northernmost town is in the rugged Ubaye valley. As a result of 19th-century immigration, its architecture and festivals have a Mexican flavour. Rooftops may see a dusting of snow as late as June.

Places to Eat

1 Le Grand Paris, Digne
MAP E2 ■ Hôtel du Grand Paris, 19 bd Thiers ■ 04 92 31 11 15 ■ Closed L Mon–Thu, Dec–Feb ■ DA ■ €€€

This restaurant at Digne's best hotel serves classic dishes with a twist.

2 Le 9, Forcalquier
MAP D3 ■ 9 av Jean Giono ■ 04 92 75 03 29 ■ Closed Apr–Sep: Wed; Oct–Mar: Tue & Wed ■ €

Close to the centre, this restaurant looks like someone's garden. It serves fresh seasonal dishes and has a terrace with lovely views over town.

3 Sens et Saveurs, Manosque
MAP D3 ■ 43 bd des Tilleuls ■ 04 92 75 00 00 ■ Closed Mon, Thu & Sun D ■ €€

Superb, creative cuisine is presented in the elegantly decorated vaulted hall of a former monastery.

Elegant interior at Sens et Saveurs

4 La Treille Muscate, Moustiers-Ste-Marie
MAP E3 ■ Pl de l'Église ■ 04 92 74 64 31 ■ Closed Wed D (and Wed L Jul), Thu, Dec, Jan, Aug ■ €€

Dine on classic dishes in a quaint restaurant by a mountain stream.

5 Ferme Ste-Cécile, Moustiers-Ste-Marie
MAP E3 ■ Rte Gorges du Verdon ■ 04 92 74 64 18 ■ Closed Sun D, Mon ■ €

Catherine and Patrick serve superb contemporary food in an 18th-century farmhouse just outside the centre.

6 Hostellerie de la Fuste, Valensole
MAP E3 ■ La Fuste ■ 04 92 72 05 95 ■ Closed Sat L, Sun D, Mon ■ DA ■ €€€

In the heart of the lavender fields award-winning meals are created from home-grown produce, fresh fish and local lamb.

7 La Caverne, Gréoux-les-Bains
MAP E3 ■ 15 Grand Rue ■ 04 92 78 19 54 ■ Closed Sun D, Mon ■ €

La Caverne may be small, with basic decor, but it is one of the best places in town for superb fresh seafood and succulent Sisteron lamb.

8 Auberge du Point Sublime, Rougon
MAP E3 ■ Point Sublime ■ 04 92 83 69 15 ■ Closed mid-Oct–Apr ■ €

The location alone would make this inn special, with a terrace gazing out at the peaks of the Canyon du Verdon, but the food is also sublime, using local produce in traditonal dishes.

9 L'Olivier, Dignes-les-Bains
MAP E2 ■ 1 rue des Monges ■ 04 92 31 47 41 ■ Closed Mon, Tue ■ €

This great little restaurant with a terrace offers great value for money. Traditional French cooking with a touch of originality.

10 Le Tivoli, Sisteron
MAP E2 ■ 21 pl Réné Cassin ■ 04 92 62 26 68 ■ Closed Wed, Thu L ■ €€

This small hotel-restaurant has an inspired young team and a great atmosphere. That, together with the top-notch meat and fish dishes, have made it the must-go place in town.

See map on p118 ←

TOP 10 Vaucluse

At the northern gates of Provence, the Vaucluse exudes a cultured air. Its rich past – Roman heritage in Orange, papal legacy in Avignon – is reflected in summer festivals in both towns, while the perched villages of the Luberon seem purpose-built for holiday homes. But the villages are not perched on a whim and Avignon's ramparts were not for show – defence was the motive for both. In the mountains and remote parts of the Luberon, you're in Provence at its most elemental.

The stunning lavender fields of the Abbaye Notre-Dame de Sénanque

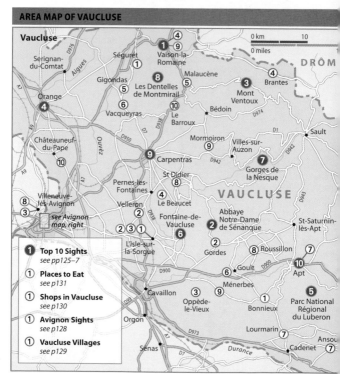

AREA MAP OF VAUCLUSE

1 Top 10 Sights
see pp125–7

1 Places to Eat
see p131

1 Shops in Vaucluse
see p130

1 Avignon Sights
see p128

1 Vaucluse Villages
see p129

1 **Vaison-la-Romaine**
One of the finest Roman towns in Provence (see pp28–9).

2 **Abbaye Notre-Dame de Sénanque**
When the lavender flowers in summer, this medieval abbey surrounded by purple fields is a spectacular sight (see pp30–31).

3 **Mont Ventoux**
MAP C2
The bald-headed "Giant of Provence" is the Vaucluse's greatest landmark; one that has inspired poets, mystics and botanists for centuries. Rising 1,900 m (6,300 ft), it commands the surrounding landscape, affording astonishing views to the sea, the Alps and the Rhône. Snowcapped in winter, the summit is revealed as arid chalk in summer and buffeted

The peak of Mont Ventoux

by strong winds all year round. The lower slopes are dense with trees, 1,000 plant varieties and wildlife.

4 **Théâtre Antique d'Orange**
MAP B2 ■ Rue Madeline Roch ■ Open daily; Apr–Sep: 9am–6pm (to 7pm Jun–Aug); Oct–Mar: 9:30am–4:30pm (to 5:30pm Mar, Oct) ■ Adm
The finest Roman theatre in Europe has its original stage wall, ensuring perfect acoustics (see p42).

5 **Parc Naturel Régional du Luberon**
MAP C3 ■ Maison du Parc, 60 pl Jean-Jaurès, Apt ■ Open 8:30am–noon, 1:30–6pm Mon–Fri (also Sat am, Easter–Sep)
The Luberon has an untamed beauty. Covering 1,500 sq km (600 sq miles), it takes in the Petit Luberon of crags, gorges and perched villages to the west and the more rounded Grand Luberon to the east. The park's headquarters have information on walks, the ecology and the area's traditions (see p50).

Roussillon cliffs in the Luberon

6 Fontaine-de-Vaucluse

MAP C3 ■ Pétrarch Library Museum: Rive gauche de la Sorgue; open Apr–Oct: Wed–Mon; adm ■ Museum d'Histoire: Chemin du Gouffre; open Apr–mid-Nov: Wed–Mon; mid-Nov–Dec, Mar: Sat–Sun; DA; adm ■ Speleology Museum: Chemin du Gouffre; open Feb–mid-Nov: daily; DA; adm

From the base of grandiose, 230-m- (750-ft-) high cliffs, Europe's most powerful spring pumps out the water which creates the River Sorgue, and attracts millions of visitors each year, as it once attracted the 14th-century Italian poet Petrarch (see p49). Downstream, the pretty village celebrates its most famous inhabitant with a museum in one of the houses he is said to have lived in. It also has two other excellent museums; one on World War II and the other on speleology.

The Sorgue at Fontaine-de-Vaucluse

7 Gorges de la Nesque

MAP C3

The Gorges de la Nesque run for 20 km (12 miles) between the villages of Villes-sur-Auzon and Monieux. The rocky drop descends more than 300 m (1,000 ft), its sides bare or covered in scrub. Cut into the cliff, the winding road is definitely not for vertigo sufferers. The Castelleras viewpoint looks onto the 850-m (2,800-ft) Rocher de Cire (Wax Rock – so-called because it is home to millions of bees). This is also the start of a testing walk to the bottom of the gorges, where Chapel St-Michel is dug into the rock.

The imposing Dentelles de Montmirail

8 Les Dentelles de Montmirail

MAP C2

Probably the prettiest mountain range in Provence, the Dentelles are formed by three ridges of chalk topped by ragged crests. The French think of these as lacework (dentelles), but they can look more like fangs in rough weather. Within the range, tiny villages (Suzette, La Roque Alric) cling to the crags as if by magic and climbers are attracted to the sheer rock faces. The walking, too, is spectacularly good, notably up to St Amand, at 730 m (2,400 ft), the highest point. Round the western edge cluster the picturesque wine villages of Beaumes-de-Venise, Gigondas, Vacqueyras and Séguret. There are marked wine routes through this picturesque vineyard region, and plenty of opportunities for tastings en route, but be sure to decide on a designated driver before you set off (see pp60–61).

THE VAUDOIS MASSACRE

The bloodiest tale in Provençal history took place in Vaucluse in 1545, when Catholic Royal authorities determined to exterminate early Protestant settlers, the Vaudois. Within weeks, as many as 3,000 were dead: women and children were burned alive and villages were destroyed. The memories, and ruins, still haunt the remoter mountainsides.

⑨ Synagogue, Carpentras
MAP C3 ■ Pl Maurice Charretier
■ **Open 10am–noon, 3–5pm Mon & Wed; 9am–noon, 2–5pm Tue & Thu, 10am–noon, 2–4pm Fri** ■ **Closed during religious services** ■ **Adm**

Expelled from France in the 14th century, the Jews sought refuge in parts of Provence then belonging to the pope. This included Carpentras, whose synagogue, founded in 1367, is the oldest still functioning on French soil. Rebuilt in the 18th century, the synagogue looks like neighbouring buildings from the outside: laws forbade decoration. Within, a monumental staircase leads to the sumptuous two-storey area of worship (men upstairs, women below), and the setting for the tabernacle, teba, candelabra and chandeliers.

The vaults of Cathédrale St-Anne

⑩ Cathédrale St-Anne, Apt
MAP C3 ■ Rue St-Anne
■ **Open 9am–1pm & 3–5pm Tue–Fri, 10:30am–noon Sat (except during religious ceremonies)**

The relics of St Anne (mother of the Virgin) were discovered on this site in 776, and here they remain, having survived the destruction of the church and its rebuilding from the 11th century on. The two crypts have also survived, containing sarcophagi from early Christian times. The cathedral has 18th-century paintings and a 15th-century stained-glass window of the Tree of Jesse. The 17th-century St Anne Chapel contains what is said to be the saint's veil, although it is probably of 9th-century Egyptian origin.

A DAY'S DRIVE IN THE VAUCLUSE MOUNTAINS

▶ MORNING

Start in Carpentras by visiting the **Synagogue**. Take the D942 to Mazan and on, through woodland, to Villes-sur-Auzon, a charming Provençal village. Continue on the D942 to the **Gorges de la Nesque** to experience 20 km (12 miles) of awe-inspiring scenery, with sheer drops of 300 m (1,000 ft). Pause at the Belvédère de Castelleras for heart-stopping views.

Continue to Monieux, stopping at Les Lavandes restaurant in the village centre *(04 90 64 05 08 • €)* if it is time for lunch and you fancy elegant, classic cooking. Continue to **Sault** where, in July and August, the valley is a riot of purple lavender, yellow broom and the white of the rocks – an unmissable sight.

AFTERNOON

Take the D164 towards **Mont Ventoux** *(see p125)*, another challenging drive, and stop for a break at the **Col des Tempêtes**. Take in the amazing views across Toulourenc Valley, then journey the summit for the most stunning panorama in Provence.

Descend the mountain to Malaucène, taking the tiny D90 into the **Dentelles de Montmirail**. Pause in any of the cafés in Beaumes-de-Venise for a glass of the local sweet white wine. Continue to delightful **Séguret** *(see p49)*, then return by the D7 to Carpentras, rewarding yourself with dinner at Le Mesclun *(rue des Poternes • 04 90 46 93 43 • €€)*, the best restaurant in town.

See map on p124–5 ←

Avignon Sights

1 Cathédrale Notre-Dame-des-Doms
MAP B3 ▪ Pl du Palais ▪ Open 8am–6pm daily (7am–7pm summer)
The medieval popes' cathedral has 17th-century alterations but a 13th-century altar.

2 Place de l'Horloge
MAP B3
Built on the old forum, the city's nerve centre is fringed with restaurants, bars and the 19th-century town hall.

3 Chartreuse du Val-de-Bénédiction
MAP B3 ▪ 58 rue de la République, Villeneuve-lez-Avignon ▪ Open Apr–Sep: 9:30am–6:30pm daily; Oct–Mar: 10am–5pm daily ▪ Closed 1 Jan, 1 May, 1 & 11 Nov, 25 Dec, 2 weeks Jan ▪ Adm
An impressive monastery and chapel with elegant gardens.

4 Musée Angladon-Dubrujeaud
MAP B3 ▪ 5 rue Laboureur ▪ Open Apr–Sep: 1–6pm Tue–Sun; Oct–Mar: 1–6pm Tue–Sat ▪ Closed 1 Jan, 25 Dec ▪ Adm
This private collection includes fabulous works by Cézanne, Manet, Picasso and Van Gogh.

5 Palais des Papes
The medieval papal palace dominates the town *(see pp12–13)*.

Panorama of the Palais des Papes

6 Pont St-Bénézet
MAP B3 ▪ Rue Ferruce ▪ Open daily; Mar: 9am–6:30pm; Apr–Jun & Sep–Oct: 9am–7pm (to 8pm Jul, to 8:30pm Aug); Nov–Feb: 9:30am–5:45pm ▪ Adm
This 13th-century bridge once had 22 arches, now it has just four *(see p38)*.

7 Rue des Teinturiers
MAP B3
This tiny street – formerly home to dye-workers – now buzzes with arty cafés and quirky boutiques.

8 Musée du Petit Palais
MAP B3 ▪ Pl du Palais ▪ Open 10am–1pm, 2–6pm Wed–Mon ▪ Closed 1 Jan, 1 May, 14 Jul, 1 Nov, 25 Dec ▪ Adm
This superb collection of medieval and Renaissance art includes an early painting by Botticelli.

9 Collection Lambert
MAP B3 ▪ Musée d'Art Contemporain, 5 rue Violette ▪ Open 11am–6pm Tue–Sun (to 7pm daily Jul–Aug) ▪ Adm
This is Avignon's premier showcase for contemporary art.

10 Musée Calvet
MAP B3 ▪ 65 rue Joseph Vernet ▪ Open 10am–1pm, 2–6pm Wed–Mon ▪ Closed 1 Jan, 1 May, 25 Dec ▪ www.musee-calvet.org ▪ Adm
The Calvet is a fine museum, with collections of paintings, sculptures and artifacts from ancient Greece to the 20th century.

Vaucluse Villages

(1) Séguret
MAP C2

This remarkably pretty medieval settlement hugs the hillside like a tight belt (see p49). Gorgeous views.

(2) Gordes
MAP C3 ■ www.gordes-village.com

Fashionable folk flock here, and no wonder. The village is perched above the Coulon Valley, and its little houses appear piled on top of one another. In the centre, the château oversees the whole with a stately Renaissance dignity.

(3) Oppède-le-Vieux
MAP C3

Flourishing in Renaissance times, Oppède was deserted by 1900 – no one wanted to live on a barely accessible rock. Now its houses are being restored by creative types, such as artists and writers, but the spot remains profoundly atmospheric, with medieval castle ruins.

(4) Brantes
MAP C2

Overhanging the gorges 550 m (1,800 ft) below, Brantes stares across the Toulourenc Valley to Mont Ventoux. Its tiny paved streets and vaulted passages boast a chapel but no shops. It is particularly impressive in March, when the almond trees are in bloom.

(5) Malaucène
MAP C2

This was where Pope Clement V had his summer residence, and it remains a grand place of 17th- and 18th-century houses, fountains and avenues shaded by plane trees.

(6) Vacqueyras
MAP B2

One of Provence's most prestigious wine villages. Admire the 11th-century church with its elegant bell tower, then go to taste the wine.

(7) Ansouis
MAP C3 ■ Château: call 04 90 77 23 36 for information on tours; adm

This village, with its labyrinthe of narrow streets, is made truly remarkable by its château, built in the 1100s and lived in by the same family until the early 2000s. The vaulted rooms, salons, armoury and kitchens are extraordinary, as are the stately gardens.

Red cliffs of Roussillon

(8) Roussillon
MAP C3

Ochre mining and erosion have fashioned the multicoloured earth into cliffs and fantastic shapes, creating a bewitching setting for a romantic perched village (see p49).

(9) Ménerbes
MAP C3

Ménerbes was superbly sited for defence. As a Protestant stronghold, it held out for five years during the 16th-century Wars of Religion. The position remains dramatic, but peace now reigns around the citadel and town houses. The views are terrific.

(10) Le Barroux
MAP C2

An eagle's nest of a village, its narrow streets lead steeply up to the splendid château at the top.

See map on pp124–5 ←

Shops in Vaucluse

① L'Isle-sur-la-Sorgue
MAP C3

Not one shop but more than 200 make this little town France's most important antiques and second-hand centre, after Paris. Grouped into seven centres, most are open Saturday to Monday, with a market on Sunday mornings. Antiques fairs are at Easter and around 15 August.

L'Isle-sur-la-Sorgue market

② Farmers' Market, Velleron
MAP C3

Provence isn't short of food markets, but this one is special. It's held in the evening and stall-holders must sell homegrown or raised produce only. It is held Monday to Saturday from 6pm, April to September, and Tuesday, Wednesday, Friday and Saturday from 4:30pm the rest of the year.

③ Les Délices du Luberon, L'Isle-sur-la-Sorgue
MAP C3 ▪ 1 av des Partage des Eaux

An unprepossessing warehouse that is full of olives, olive preparations and olive derivatives such as tapenade or *melet* (a blend of fennel, peppers, olives and anchovies).

④ Lou Canesteou, Vaison-la-Romaine
MAP C2 ▪ 10 rue Raspail

Josiane Déal personally selects the 160 varieties of artisanal cheese for her shop, and has been named a *Meilleur Ouvrier* ("Master of her Craft") for her expertise.

⑤ Les Olivades, Avignon
MAP B3 ▪ 56 rue Joseph Vernet

This company has been producing and printing Provençal fabrics since 1818. It's now the only such outfit in the region, with materials, table linen and wedding gowns.

⑥ Edith Mézard, Lumières Goult
MAP C3 ▪ Château de l'Ange

The little château near Goult is a perfect setting for beautifully embroidered clothes and a great range of linen for the house.

⑦ Confiserie Artisanale Denis Ceccon, Apt
MAP C3 ▪ 60 quai de la Liberté

Apt is the world capital of crystallized fruit, and Denis Ceccon is one of the few remaining artisans to work by traditional methods – try his apricots.

⑧ Nougats Silvain, St Didier
MAP C3 ▪ Rte de Vénasque St Didier

This is a farming and fruit-growing family known for their own delicious nougat. Don't miss their honey either.

⑨ Château Pesquié, Mormoiron
MAP C2 ▪ Rte de Flassan

The château has lovely grounds and first-rate Ventoux wines.

⑩ Chocolaterie Bernard Castelain, Châteauneuf-du-Pape
MAP B3 ▪ Rte de Sorgues

Another warehouse – this time packed with a dazzling array of chocolate. Enter only if you have iron self-control.

Chocolaterie Bernard Castelain

Places to Eat

PRICE CATEGORIES

For a three-course meal for one with half a bottle of wine (or equivalent meal), taxes and extra charges.

€ under €40 €€ €40–€60 €€€ over €60

1 La Bastide de Capelongue, Bonnieux

MAP C3 ■ Rue du Temple ■ 04 90 75 89 78 ■ Closed Tue L, Wed, mid-Jan–early Mar, 2 weeks Dec ■ €€€

Chef Edouard Loubet is known for aromatic Provençal cuisine, using his own herbs for dishes such as rack of lamb smoked with wild thyme.

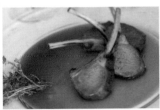

Lamb at La Bastide de Capelongue

2 Café des Fleurs, L'Isle-sur-la-Sorgue

MAP C3 ■ 9 rue Théodore Aubanel ■ 04 90 20 66 94 ■ Closed Tue, Wed (excl mid-Jun–Aug), Jan ■ DA ■ €€

Delicious Provençal food served in a stylish dining room or on a shady patio. Go on a Sunday, when the town has a busy market.

3 Hiely-Lucullus, Avignon

MAP B3 ■ 5 rue de la République ■ 04 90 86 17 07 ■ Closed Tue, Wed ■ €€

One of Avignon's oldest restaurants, which adds a wonderful lightness of touch to its classic dishes.

4 Auberge du Beaucet, Le Beaucet

MAP C3 ■ 04 90 66 10 82 ■ Closed Mon, Tue–Sat L, Sun D, Dec–Jan ■ €€

The hamlet is remote but the refined Provençal cooking is a treat – try the snail ravioli. Booking is essential.

5 Les Florets, Gigondas

MAP B2 ■ Rte des Dentelles ■ 04 90 65 85 01 ■ Closed Wed, Thu L, Jan–mid-Mar ■ €€

The panoramic terrace has superb views of the Dentelles de Montmirail, and the regional cuisine is matched by an excellent wine list.

6 Christian Etienne, Avignon

MAP B3 ■ 10 rue de Mons ■ 04 90 86 16 50 ■ Closed Wed–Thu, mid-Oct ■ €€€

Frescoes, a terrace and superb Provençal fare – the chef is especially good with truffles and tomatoes.

7 Auberge de la Fenière, Lourmarin

MAP C3 ■ Rte de Cadenet ■ 04 90 68 11 79 ■ Closed Mon, Tue (Jul & Aug: open D), mid-Nov–early Feb ■ DA ■ €€

Reine Sammut, one of France's rare female top chefs, brings international influence to regional cuisine.

8 Le Prieuré, Villeneuve-les-Avignon

MAP B3 ■ 7 pl de Chapitre ■ 04 90 15 90 15 ■ Closed Nov–Mar ■ DA ■ €€€

The locally sourced menu changes four times a week, offering gourmet cuisine in a heavenly setting.

9 Moulin à Huile, Vaison-la-Romaine

MAP C2 ■ 1 quai du Maréchal Foch ■ 04 90 36 04 56 ■ Closed Sun D, Mon–Wed ■ €€€

Superb setting in the medieval part of town. New owners prepare superb regional dishes for a set menu.

10 La Fourchette, Avignon

MAP B3 ■ 17 rue Racine ■ 04 90 85 20 93 ■ Closed Sat, Sun, 3 wks Aug ■ €€

Much favoured by Avignon locals for its country-inn style and treatment of Provençal classics, like sumptuous *boeuf en daube* (*see p67*).

See map on pp124–5

Streetsmart

Colourful façades of houses in the city of Orange, Vaucluse

Getting To and Around Provence and the Côte d'Azur

Arriving by Air

Nice Côte d'Azur Airport is the best gateway for Provence, with frequent flights from Paris, London, New York, Dubai and other major cities. Buses run the 7 km (4.5 miles) to central Nice every 15 minutes. A taxi to the centre costs around €35. Other direct airport buses serve Antibes, Cannes and Monaco.

Marseille-Provence Airport is situated 27 km (17 miles) northwest of Marseille and 24 km (15 miles) southeast of Aix-en-Provence. Taxis to both destinations cost around €50. Buses run to Marseille-St-Charles railway station about every 15 minutes, with numerous other direct buses to Aix-en-Provence, St-Tropez and inland Provence.

Both airports are served by **Air France, easyJet** and dozens of smaller low-cost airlines.

Arriving by Train

Every major town in Provence is connected by high-speed TGV trains, run by the French rail operator **SNCF**, and there are also links from many Provençal cities to Paris. It is a 3-hour journey from the French capital to Marseille, Avignon or Aix-en-Provence.

Eurostar services run directly from London to Avignon and Marseille, the latter a 6.5 hour service. The TGV runs to Barcelona in 4 hours. Additional **Thello** services link Marseille, Cannes, Antibes, Nice and Monaco to Genoa and Milan. Be aware that Avignon and Aix-en-Provence have airport-style TGV stations, each one just a short bus ride from the town centre.

Arriving by Road

Avignon, Aix-en-Provence, Marseille and Nice are connected to Europe's largest cities by the **Eurolines** long-distance coach service. The national bus company **Isilines** has a wide network across France at very reasonable prices. Bear in mind that travelling by train or plane is almost certainly quicker than travelling by bus, and that the Paris Gallieni coach interchange station is a rough and ready affair.

The drive from Paris to Provence is an easy one, except at the start or end of French holiday periods. Allow at least 6 hours for the 700-km (435-mile) journey to Avignon via the A6 Autoroute du Soleil, including about €55 in tolls. From Paris to Nice allow 10 hours plus around €75 in tolls. There are rest stops, or *aires*, every 30 km (20 miles) or so. Most have picnic tables and public toilets.

Travelling by Train

Provence is a vast geographical region covered by mountains, lakes and rolling fields of lavender. Fortunately, one of the world's best rail services, SNCF, runs from Arles and Nîmes in the west to Nice and Monaco in the east, connecting every major town by high-speed TGV. Even tiny villages are linked by less frequent TER local trains that often run from south to north up to Grasse, Digne and Orange. The **Train des Pignes** is another key line. This historic route runs from Nice's Gare de Provence to Digne-les-Bains in the Haut-Alpes through splendid Alpine scenery. Several walking trails begin at stations en route. The **Train des Merveilles** is another pretty route of great attraction to hikers. Its route traverses what was Italian territory until 1947, past the towns of Tende and Sospel.

By Car

Provençal roads offer drivers and passengers breathtaking vistas of vineyards, canyons and mountains, making for a magnificent journey. That said, a car is essential only in certain areas, such as the Gorges du Verdon and rural areas around Vaison-la-Romaine and Abbaye de Sénanque. It is not recommended to drive in any major regional city. There, even local residents prefer to use public transport when getting about. All the main car hire companies have offices in Provençal towns. A novel addition is Nice's all-electric car share scheme **Auto Bleue**.

By Bus

Buses in Provence are best used for local or intercity trips – the trains cover longer distances. Numerous companies operate from town bus stations *(gares routières)*. Smaller villages, coastal resorts and rural areas are connected by small bus routes.

By Taxi

Taxis are reliable and use meters *(compteurs)* but are not usually flagged down on the street. Find one at a taxi rank, book by phone or ask your hotel to call one. Be aware that taxis in regional cities and towns are very expensive.

By Bicycle

Each July, the region's stunning landscape is beamed across the world as cameras follow the Tour de France cycle race.

Professional bike tour outfits like Nice's **Azur Cycle** and Provence's **Cycling for Softies** cover many of the same routes, and include the Côte d'Azur and the Luberon's lavender fields. Bicycle share schemes similar to those in Paris and London are in operation in all regional cities. Register online then grab a bike from Avignon's **Vélopop**, Aix-en-Provence's **Cycle Sud**, Nice's **Vélobleu** or Marseille's **Le Vélo**.

By Public Transport

France has some of the best public transport in Europe. Getting around the region's cities by bus, tram and (in Marseille) metro or boat presents few problems. Fares are integrated, so a single ticket can be used on any combination of transport for 1 hour. Day passes and books of tickets *(carnets)* are also available.

By Boat and Ferry

Boats are a great way to take a day trip along the coast. Most useful are the **Trans Côte d'Azur** ferries from Cannes to the Iles de Lérins, and **Bateaux Verts** from Ste-Maxime to St-Tropez. Boat tours are also run around Avignon and into the Camargue.

On Foot

Provence is superb walking country, offering guided or marked walks around historic cities and along the coast. *Sentiers balisés* are the local trails, while *sentiers de grande randonnée* are long-distance hiking tracks, and both are part of a vast network that covers all of France. The main long-distance trails are the GR5, GR51 GR6 and GR9. Maps and guides are available from tourist offices.

DIRECTORY

ARRIVING BY AIR

Air France
🌐 airfrance.fr

easyJet
🌐 easyjet.com

Marseille-Provence Airport
📞 0820 81 14 14
🌐 marseille-airport.com

Nice Côte d'Azur Airport
📞 0820 42 33 33
🌐 nice.aeroport.fr

ARRIVING BY RAIL

Eurostar
🌐 eurostar.com

SNCF
🌐 voyages-sncf.com

Thello
🌐 thello.com

Train des Merveilles
🌐 tendemerveilles.com

Train des Pignes
🌐 trainprovence.com

ARRIVING BY ROAD

Eurolines
🌐 eurolines.com

Isilines
🌐 isilines.fr

TRAVELLING BY CAR

Auto Bleue
🌐 auto-bleue.org

Europcar
🌐 europcar.com

French autoroutes
🌐 autoroutes.fr

Sixt
🌐 sixt.com

CYCLING

Azur Cycle
🌐 azurcycletours.com

Cycle Sud
🌐 cyclesud.fr

Cycling for Softies
🌐 cycling-for-softies.co.uk

Le Vélo
🌐 levelo-mpm.fr

Vélobleu
🌐 velobleu.org

Vélopop
🌐 velopop.fr

BOAT AND FERRY

Bateau Verts
🌐 bateauxverts.com

Trans Côte d'Azur
🌐 trans-cote-azur.com

Practical Information

Passports and Visas

Visitors from outside the European Economic Area (EEA), European Union (EU) and Switzerland need a valid passport to enter France. EEA, EU and Swiss nationals can use their national identity cards instead. Citizens of Canada, the US, Australia and New Zealand can visit France for up to 90 days without a visa as long as their passport is valid for 6 months beyond the date of entry. For longer stays, a visa is necessary and must be obtained in advance from the French Embassy in their home country. Most other non-EU nationals need a visa, and should consult the **French Foreign Ministry** website for information. Schengen visas are valid for France.

Travel Safety Advice

Visitors can get up-to-date safety information from the Foreign and Commonwealth Office (FCO) in the UK, the State Department in the US and the Department of Foreign Affairs and Trade in Australia.

Customs and Immigration

For EU citizens there is no limit on most goods taken into or out of France, as long as the items are for personal use. Exceptions include some types of food, some plants and all endangered species. Non-EU citizens may import 200 cigarettes and a litre of spirits per adult, and can claim back VAT on EU purchases over €25. This can be done at Nice or Marseille airport when leaving the EU.

Travel Insurance

All travellers are advised to buy insurance against accidents, illness, theft, loss and travel delays or cancellations. France has a reciprocal health agreement with other EU countries, and EU citizens will receive emergency treatment under the French healthcare system on production of a valid European Health Insurance Card (EHIC). Prescriptions must be paid for upfront. Non-EU visitors should check if their country has any similar arrangements with France. Car-hire agencies offer vehicle cover, although this may already be covered under other travel or home insurance policies.

Health

Provence has no serious health risks. Pharmacies act as the first line of France's medical service. Highly trained pharmacists can give advice and offer prescriptions. Pharmacies are marked with a large green cross and are usually open from 9am to 8pm Monday to Saturday. When closed, there will be a sign in the window giving the location of the nearest *pharmacie du nuit*, which will be open. In all towns one pharmacy will open at night and weekends. Some pharmacies are open 24/7, including **Pharmacie Masséna** in Nice. **SOS Médecins**, the 24-hour medical service, can send a paramedic or a doctor. If you need an ambulance, dial the **SAMU** number. Fire stations also have ambulances and are qualified to do first aid.

Dentists are listed in the *Pages Jaunes* (Yellow Pages) under *Dentistes*.

Personal Security

Theft from cars, bags and luggage is as prevalent along the Côte d'Azur as it is in any populous tourist area. The police have a strong presence along the coast. That said, do not risk taking valuables, passports, tickets or more cash than you need to the beach.

To report a theft, go to the *commissariat de police*. These are listed in the phone book, or call the **Préfecture Centrale** for details (open 24 hours a day). All crimes should be reported, if only for insurance purposes. For lost property look online for the *objets trouvés* office in the relevant town.

Violent crime is far less common, but take the same precautions as you would at home. Female travellers will feel comfortable across the region, even when alone. Gay and lesbian travellers can relax as France, and in particular the Côte d'Azur towns of Nice, Cannes and St-Tropez, are among the most liberal places in the world.

Disabled Travellers

The main towns and cities in Provence offer excellent access for people with a disability. Admission is free to blind people in most major museums and art galleries in Nice, Avignon and Marseille. Most have audio and Braille guides in English. The best source of information on disabled facilities in France is the **Association des Paralysés de France (APF)**. This organization produces an annual Guide Vacances holiday booklet, which is downloadable as a PDF from their website. **Access Travel** offers wheelchair-accessible properties that have been inspected or suggested by a wheelchair user. They also offer airfares world-wide, and will liaise with airlines to arrange services. The website **YoureAble** has travel forums covering all aspects of your holiday. Free or reduced-rate transport is available in Nice and Marseille for people with disabilities and their carers. **SNCF** French Railways offers the **Accès Plus** service and has an accessibility helpline. For wheelchair access to trains, book 48 hours in advance. All train stations can provide a boarding ramp. **SOS Voyageurs** offers help to disabled travellers in Marseille and Nice. Most restaurants and many older hotels have – at the very best – limited access for wheelchair users. It is advisable to phone ahead to check the situation before booking.

Driving Licences

All valid full European, Australian, Canadian and US driving licences are accepted in France. It is recommended that non-EU visitors get an International Driving Permit (IDP), even though North Americans do not need one. To hire a car, you will also need a credit card and your passport.

DIRECTORY

PASSPORTS AND VISAS

French Foreign Ministry
w diplomatie.gouv.fr

EMBASSIES AND CONSULTATES

Australia
4 rue Jean Rey, Paris
C 01 40 59 33 00
w france.embassy.gov.au

Canada
MAP Q4 ■ 10 rue Lamartine, Nice
C 04 93 92 93 22
w canadainternational.gc.ca

Ireland
MAP G4 ■ 69 av du Roi Albert, Cannes C 01 44 17 67 00 w dfa.ie

New Zealand
103, rue de Grenelle, Paris
C 01 45 01 43 43
w mfat.govt.nz

UK
MAP M6 ■ 24 avenue du Prado, Marseille
C 04 91 15 72 10
w gov.uk

USA
MAP L5 ■ pl Varian Fry, Marseille
C 01 43 12 48 85
w marseille.usconsulate.gov

TRAVEL SAFETY

Australia
w dfat.gov.au
w smarttraveller.gov.au

UK
Foreign and Commonwealth Office
w gov.uk/foreign-travel-advice

USA
w travel.state.gov

HEALTH AND SAFETY

Pharmacie Masséna, Nice
MAP Q4 ■ 7 av Masséna
C 04 93 87 78 94

Prefecture Centrale
C 01 53 71 53 71

SOS Médecins
C 3624
w sosmedecins-france.fr

EMERGENCY SERVICES

Ambulance (SAMU)
C 15

Any Emergency
C 112

Fire Department
C 18

Police
C 17

DISABLED TRAVELLERS

Access Travel
w access-travel.co.uk

APF
w apf.asso.fr

SNCF Accès Plus
C 3635
(say "Access Plus")
w accessibilite.sncf.com

SOS Voyageurs
C 04 93 16 02 61 (Nice)
C 04 91 62 12 80 (Marseille)
w rivch0.wix.com/sosvoyageurs

YoureAble
w youreable.com

Currency and Banking

France uses the euro (€), which is divided into 100 cents. Paper notes are in denominations of €5, €10, €20, €50, €100, €200 and €500. Coins are €2, €1, 50c, 20c, 10c, 5c, 2c and 1c. ATMs (cash machines) are the easiest way to get cash out and are also a good way to beat commission charges. Surcharges depend on your bank. For the best rates, don't give the ATM the option of converting euros into your home currency, as the rate is always poor. Few banks offer currency exchange facilities these days, and bureaux de change are also few and far between. Pre-paid currency cards (cash passports) are a secure way of carrying money. They can be pre-loaded with euros, fixing exchange rates before you leave, and used like a debit card. Credit cards are widely accepted, but there may be a minimum charge. If your credit card is lost or stolen, inform the police and your credit card company.

Internet and Telephone

Many cafés, hotels and restaurants offer free Wi-Fi. So do many towns across the region, by way of hotspots in key areas.

The dialling code for France is 00 33. Phone numbers must always be dialled in full, including the regional code, which most often starts with 04. Mobile phones cost a little extra to call, and numbers start with 06. Although it's not as expensive as it once was to make and receive calls in France from abroad, downloading data using 4G rather than Wi-Fi can be exorbitant. Using Skype for calls and WhatsApp for messaging should also reduce your mobile phone bill.

Consider buying a local SIM card or a pay-as-you-go mobile (both widely available) to avoid high roaming charges, but note these charges are due to be abolished for EU travellers from 2017.

Postal Services

Most post offices are open from 9am–noon and 2–5pm Monday–Friday and 9am–noon on Saturday. Avoid queues by using the multilingual stamp machines in most post offices. Stamps for postcards are sold in any tobacconist (tabac).

Television and Media

Most hotels subscribe to multilingual cable and satellite channels, which vary the diet of French-language entertainment. TF1 shows an array of silly game shows amid serious news in French. Arte offers more cultural productions and vivid documentaries.

The English-language International New York Times is available in most resorts and train station newsagents in cities on day of publication, as are The Times, The Guardian and others. **Nice-Matin** is an easy-to-understand local paper published along the Côte d'Azur. It features an excellent events pullout section all summer. **Riviera Radio** beams global hits and English-language news from its base in Monaco on 106.5 FM, and online.

Opening Hours

In general, big stores and supermarkets open from 8am–7pm, plus 9am–1pm on Sundays. Convenience stores stay open later. Banks and businesses are generally open 9am–5:30pm, with a generous two-hour break for lunch from around 12:30pm. Even in smaller villages, locals expect to be able to purchase their daily essentials from a boulangerie, tabac and newsagent every day.

Museums have similar opening hours across the entire region. Almost all are open from 10am–6pm Tuesday–Sunday. Outdoor cultural sights stay open later in summer.

Public holidays include New Year's Day, Easter Monday, 1 May (Labour Day), 8 May (VE Day), Ascension Day (40 days after Easter), Whitsun (7th Sunday after Easter), Whit Monday (the day after Whitsun), 14 July (Bastille Day), 15 August (Assumption), 1 November (All Saints' Day), 11 November (Armistice Day) and 25 December (Christmas Day).

Time Difference

France operates on Central European Time (CET), which is 1 hour ahead of Greenwich Mean Time (GMT), 6 hours ahead of US Eastern Standard Time (EST) and 9 hours ahead of Pacific Standard Time (PST).

The clock moves forward by one hour during European Daylight Savings Time, which runs from the last Sunday in March until the last Sunday in October.

Electrical Appliances

France uses plugs with two round pins and an electrical voltage and frequency of 230V/50Hz. North American, British and Australian devices will need adaptors, which are readily available in most French supermarkets, but can also be bought ahead of travel or at the airport.

Weather

The South of France, and especially the Côte d'Azur, is justly famed for having one of most desirable climates on the planet. The coastal stretches from Monaco to Cannes bathe in up to 300 days of sun per year. Pleasant breezes keep most of the sweltering summer heat at bay during the busy months of July and August, although visitors should be prepared for an occasional week-long heat wave, which makes sightseeing a little more arduous. Temperatures in May, June, September and October usually hover around 25°C (77°F). Restaurant terraces will be busy but fewer crowds descend upon the region's cultural sights. November and March can be rainy. The sunshine makes even midwinter a terrific time to visit, but bear in mind that Mistral winds can bring icy weather to Marseille and inland Provence.

Language

English is widely spoken by people working in coastal resorts, tourist offices, hotels, larger restaurants and airports. It is less fluently spoken in urban Marseille and in rural communities, where you will need a grasp of French in order to be understood. Etiquette is valued even higher than linguistic ability: shake hands on being introduced and use the titles "Monsieur" and "Madame" on greeting.

Visitor Information

Multilingual staff can offer advice on where to visit, and hand out a wealth of maps and brochures, at every well-stocked Office de Tourisme in Provence and the Côte d'Azur. As you might expect from the world's most visited nation, even the tiniest town has an informative, all-encompassing website with sightseeing ideas and accommodation information in several languages. Those of larger cities, such as Nice, offer a selection of tourism, transport and children's apps, plus downloadable PDF brochures for elderly, or disabled travellers.

The wider official web portals for **VisitProvence** and **Côte d'Azur Tourisme** offer tempting tourism ideas from sea-kayaking in the Camargue to vineyard visits in the Var. For a literary introduction of the region, try classics such as Peter Mayle's *A Year in Provence*, James Morgan's *Chasing Matisse* or Carol Drinkwater's *Olive Farm* series.

Things to Avoid

For two weeks in May it becomes impossible to get a hotel room or a table in a good restaurant in or around Cannes as the resort hosts its Film Festival. The same is true of Monaco when the Rallye Monte Carlo (Jan) and Monaco Grand Prix (dates vary) take place.

August sees long delays on the roads to and around the south – avoid the first and last weekends.

Provence has its share of pests, from mosquitoes to jellyfish, and beware of spiky sea urchins when walking on rocky shores.

Trips and Tours

Such a range of organized trips exist in this region that a visit to each town's tourist office or website is the best place to start. **Hop-on-hop-off Buses** circle the major sights of Nice and Marseille, while walking tours and *petit trains* cover Avignon, Aix and Antibes, and other smaller cities. As well as the various city bike-share schemes, bespoke cycle tours of Provence are available, including **Cyclomundo** and **Provence Cycling**.

Each town's highlight will also have a tour to suit. For example, **Local Avignon Tours** visits the local lavender fields and Roman sights, while **Avignon Gourmet Tours** will take you round the markets and to sample the local Châteauneuf-du-Pape wine. **Levantin**, in the port of Marseille, is one of Europe's largest catamarans, offering cruises round the Frioul Islands and the Calanques National Park. **Mobilboard Segway Tours** run through pedestrianized Vieux Nice. Vintage Solex motorbikes (Brigitte Bardot was a fan) can be hired, along with a guide, in **Juan-les-Pins**. **Guided Tours of St-Paul-de-Vence** also offers arty walks in the footsteps of one-time resident, painter Marc Chagall.

Most rural areas also have their own organized tours. Try **Provence Wine Tours** for tasting trips into the Lubéron vineyards, while **Esterel Aventure** offers off-roading buggy and jeep trips over the rocky bluffs between Cannes and St-Tropez.

Shopping

The South of France is a place to shop 'til you drop. You may not bag a bargain – Tropezienne sandals from St-Tropez are far from cheap – but local finds abound. Bars of *savon du Marseille* soap make great gifts and come perfumed with olive oil, lavender and other scents. Glass has been blown in Biot for centuries, and its glassware graces every smart table on the Côte d'Azur. A dozen AOP wine appellations span the region, with top vintages on sale at the airports of Nice and Marseille.

Daily markets grace most mid-size towns from Cannes' Marché Forville to Avignon's Marché des Halles. Other towns have a weekly market day – the most colourful of these are Arles' Saturday morning market alongside the old ramparts, and St-Tropez's Tuesday market in place des Lices.

For antiques, pay a visit to St-Rémy's Wednesday market or the *brocantes* of Isle sur la Sorgue, or head to the Quartier des Antiquaires in Nice, which boasts the third-highest concentration of antiques shops in France.

Follow the trail of the region's most famous artists to find the finest galleries. The proximity of the Fondation Maeght makes St-Paul-de-Vence a haven for contemporary art. Picasso's sojourn in Vallauris restarted that town's ceramic trade, which continues to this day. Aix was home to Cézanne and Arles to Van Gogh, and both have several exceptional galleries.

Food is a shopping trip all to itself. Most items can be jarred, wrapped or vacuum-sealed for the trip home. Olive oil makes a great purchase, as do locally made olive wood trays and chopping boards. Jams from Menton's citrus orchards, *calisson* candies from Aix and dried mushrooms from the inland Var are easily transportable, as are genuine herbes de Provence.

Eating and Drinking

Whether you are looking for local market produce or a Michelin-starred feast, there are options to suit every visitor's tastes and budget.

In the east of the region, the cuisine has humble origins. Niçoise dishes use a medley of local fish, offcuts of meat (as used in its *daube* oxtail stew) and simple, fresh ingredients such as those found in salade Niçoise.

In Marseille the diet is also drawn from the sea. *Bouillabaisse*, a hearty fish stew, is a must-eat served in locations around the Vieux Port. *Tajine aux poissons* is a fishy dish reflecting Marseille's North African influence.

In inland Provence it's a different matter. Rich cities such as Avignon feast on pigeon and pork, as well as delicious lamb from the Sisteron hills.

For picnics, *boulangeries* (bakeries) and *pâtisseries* (cake shops) sell a choice of loaves, rolls and pastries. Head for the *traiteur* or *charcuterie* to buy cuts of cold meat and patés or ready-made quiches and salads.

Provence's unique takeaway snack is *pan bagnat*, a crusty roll soaked with olive oil and stuffed with *salade Niçoise*.

Vegetarians will dine excellently in Provence, with a range of salads, omelettes, cheeses, hearty stews, local pastas and Asian cuisine. Supermarkets are increasingly stocking gluten-free and special diet options, too.

Most restaurants have several set menus, the cheapest lunch offering usually starting as low as €15. If you are not sure what to order, these offer excellent value. Eating *à la carte* (selecting each dish yourself) is usually more expensive. Dining hours are usually noon–2pm (with final food orders at 1:30pm) and then from 7:30pm onwards.

Water as well as wine is always drunk with meals and, even in upmarket restaurants, it's common to ask for a *carafe d'eau* (jug of tap water) rather than a more expensive bottle of mineral water.

In cafés the bill for each drink is brought to your table with your order but there is no need to pay until you leave. A tip is customary. In restaurants, a 10 per cent gratuity for good service is usual. Most places are child-friendly and will usually provide a high chair and a children's menu.

Provence is home to some of the world's best restaurants. If you plan to dine in one, be sure to book well in advance. Casual attire is usually acceptable, but top establishments may ask for jacket and tie for men.

Where to Stay

Hotels are the mainstay of guest accommodation in Provence. Budget options include the **Formule 1** and **B&B Hôtels** no-frills chains. You might also choose to skip the hotel breakfast, which is almost always extra and can be disappointing. **Chambres d'hôtes** are another story. These homestays offer bed-and-breakfast in the traditional sense. A hearty breakfast will be prepared by the owner, and you may well eat with your hosts and other guests.

You can also opt for a less expensive stay in a rented apartment. **Nice Pebbles** is the market leader for holiday rental accommodation in Nice, with over 170 smart apartments in the city, each equipped with Wi-Fi, fine linens and other luxuries. They also manage chic properties in Antibes, Cannes and Villefranche. Alternatively, **Airbnb** offers thousands of apartments and rooms across the region.

Camping France lists every camp site in the area. These range from huge operations with fixed tents and static caravans to eco-friendly and ever popular "glamping".

Rates and Booking

Rates vary phenomenally across the seasons with mid-August prices often tripling those in March or October. Booking online in advance almost always guarantees the best rate. For the best deal, check prices on the hotel's own website, as well as on the major booking websites.

Places to Stay

PRICE CATEGORIES
For a standard, double room per night (with breakfast if included), taxes and extra charges.

€ under €200 €€ 200–400 €€€ over €400

Luxury Resorts

Hôtel la Baie Dorée, Antibes

MAP G4 ■ 579 bd de la Garoupe ■ 04 93 67 30 67 ■ www.baiedoree.com ■ €€

With only 15 rooms – all but two of which have a view of the sea – this hotel is an intimate alternative to the usual large-scale luxury resorts found on the Riviera. It has a private beach and a jetty with loungers set around a tiny harbour.

Le Byblos, St-Tropez

MAP F5 ■ Av Paul Signac ■ 04 94 56 68 00 ■ Closed Nov–Mar ■ www.byblos. com ■ DA ■ €€€

Beloved of rock stars and fashionistas, Le Byblos also has one of St-Trop's trendiest nightspots, Les Caves du Roy (see p92), attached to it. There's also a Sisley spa and an Alain Ducasse restaurant. Decked out in Art Deco colours worthy of a chic fashion shoot, this is among the most luxurious hotels in Provence.

Cap d'Estel, Eze

MAP H4 ■ 1312 av Raymond Poincaré, Èze ■ 04 93 76 29 29 ■ www. capestel.com ■ DA ■ €€€

Constructed in 1900 on a secluded peninsula with a private beach, the Cap d'Estel is much-loved by A-listers for its pampering and privacy.

Rooms are in four buildings amid an exotic garden with a spectacular infinity pool.

Martinez, Cannes

MAP G4 ■ 73 bd de la Croisette ■ 04 93 90 12 34 ■ www.cannes-martinez.grand.hyatt. com ■ DA ■ €€€

A landmark on Cannes' esplanade, the Martinez is a triumph of fin-de-siècle wedding-cake stucco architecture, with a private beach. Part of the Hyatt chain of luxury hotels, it has everything you could want for a sybaritic stay.

Monte Carlo Beach Hotel, Roquebrune-Cap-Martin

MAP H3 ■ Av Princesse-Grace ■ 04 93 28 66 66 ■ www.monte-carlo-beach.com ■ DA ■ €€€

This 46-room Art Deco showpiece hotel has an Olympic-sized pool, a crescent of private beach, three fine restaurants and an overall ambience of exclusive luxury and comfort.

Résidence de la Pinede, St-Tropez

MAP F5 ■ Plage de la Bouillabaisse ■ 04 94 55 91 00 ■ Closed mid-Oct–mid-Apr ■ www. residencepinede.com ■ DA ■ €€€

With its private beach, pool, fine sea views and excellent location, it is

hardly surprising that this is a favourite with those who know St-Tropez well.

Grand Hotels

Grand Hôtel Nord-Pinus, Arles

MAP B4 ■ 17 pl du Forum ■ Closed mid-Nov–mid-Mar ■ 04 90 93 44 44 ■ www.nord-pinus.com ■ DA ■ €€

This historic hotel is the best address in Arles. The lounge and foyer have traditional Provençal decor.

Hôtel d'Europe, Avignon

MAP B3 ■ 12 pl Crillon ■ 04 90 14 76 76 ■ www. heurope.com ■ €€

Step back in time as you enter the ornate gates of this beautiful, historic hotel. Heavy wooden furniture and antique tapestries create an elegant atmosphere, and no request is too much for the impeccable staff.

Hôtel Hermitage, Monte Carlo

MAP H4 ■ Sq Beau-marchais ■ 00 377 98 06 40 00 ■ www.hotel-hermitagemontecarlo. com ■ €€

The Hermitage recalls the splendour of *belle époque* Monaco, with its glass-domed atrium where breakfast is served, the dazzlingly over-the-top restaurant decorated in pink and gold, and the large marble terrace. A monument in its own right, it is one of Europe's smartest hotels – a reputation it has held for more than 100 years.

Le Negresco, Nice
MAP P5 ▪ 37 prom des Anglais ▪ 04 93 16 64 00 ▪ www.hotel-negresco-nice.com ▪ DA ▪ €€
The flagship of the whole Riviera, the Negresco is the grandest of grand hotels, from its splendid *belle époque* façade to its immaculate rooms and attentive service. One of the world's most opulent hotels.

Carlton Inter-Continental, Cannes
MAP G4 ▪ 58 La Croisette ▪ 04 93 06 40 06 ▪ www.intercontinental-carlton-cannes.com ▪ DA ▪ €€€
The Carlton is a Cannes landmark, home of the stars during the Film Festival and appropriately luxurious, with its private beach and high standards of service. Although part of an international chain, it nonetheless retains an individual character.

Hôtel du Cap-Eden-Roc, Antibes
MAP G4 ▪ Bd Kennedy ▪ 04 93 61 39 01 ▪ www.hotel-du-cap-eden-roc.com ▪ DA ▪ €€€
As ostentatious as the Negresco in its way, the Eden Roc is another landmark of the Riviera and has been for more than a century. It offers exclusivity and film-star chic in tropical gardens and is, in a word, idyllic.

Hôtel de Paris, Monte Carlo
MAP H4 ▪ Pl du Casino ▪ 00 377 98 06 30 00 ▪ www.hoteldeparis-montecarlo.com ▪ DA ▪ €€€
Rivalling the Hermitage for *belle époque* splendour, the Hôtel de Paris has a famous café-terrace on the ground floor *(see p110)* and is very close to the casino *(see pp32–3)*. Queen Victoria stayed here, as have a host of other crowned heads and celebrities.

Hôtel Royal Riviera, Jean-Cap-Ferrat
MAP H4 ▪ 3 av Jean Monnet ▪ 04 93 76 31 00 ▪ www.royal-riviera.com ▪ DA ▪ €€€
This luxurious 1904 hotel is situated on its private beach on the Cap Ferrat peninsula. The rooms are distributed between the main building and the Orangerie. All of them are spacious with modern amenities, and many have sea views. The superb restaurant has a terrace and there's a heated pool.

La Réserve, Beaulieu
MAP H4 ▪ 5 bd du Maréchal Leclerc ▪ 04 93 01 00 01 ▪ www.reserve-beaulieu.com ▪ DA ▪ €€€
Opened in the late 19th century, this pink palace in its semi-tropical grounds is a grand place to stay. It still retains the glory of its 1920s heyday and exudes an air of quietly indulgent luxury.

Château Hotels

Château de Trigance, Trigance
MAP F3 ▪ 04 94 76 91 18 ▪ Closed Nov–Mar ▪ www.chateau-de-trigance.fr ▪ No air conditioning ▪ €
With just 10 rooms this small château, built in the 10th century and painstakingly restored by its owners over the last 30 years, is now a great three-star hotel. The rooms have four-poster beds and medieval-style decor, and the restaurant is excellent.

Château des Alpilles, St-Rémy
MAP B3 ▪ RD 31 ▪ 04 90 92 03 33 ▪ www.chateau-desalpilles.com ▪ €€
The château was built in the 19th century for a prominent Arles family. Service and cuisine rate highly, and the rooms in the castle, former chapel and converted farmhouses are beautifully decorated.

Château Eza, Èze
MAP H4 ▪ Rue de la Pise ▪ 04 93 41 12 24 ▪ www.chateaueza.com ▪ €€
A wonderful collection of medieval buildings now converted into a hotel. Rooms are luxuriously decorated with opulent Oriental rugs and lush marble bathrooms.

Château de la Pioline, Aix-en-Provence
MAP C4 ▪ 260 rue Guillaume Du Vair Pole ▪ 04 42 52 27 27 ▪ DA ▪ www.chateaudelapioline.com ▪ €€
This elegant 16th-century château is just 3 km (2 miles) from Aix. It combines historical detail with modern amenities. Some smaller rooms are in a garden outbuilding.

Château de Valmer, La Croix Valmer
MAP F5 ▪ 04 94 55 15 15 ▪ Closed Oct–Apr ▪ www.chateauvalmer.com ▪ No air conditioning ▪ €€
Surrounded by a 5-ha (12-acre) park with palm trees and a vineyard, this hotel even has its own private beach.

Hôtel du Petit Palais, Nice

MAP P4 ▪ 17 av Emile Bieckert ▪ 04 93 62 19 11 ▪ www.petitpalaisnice. com ▪ DA ▪ €€
Set in an extensive garden, this former palace offers a quiet and scenic retreat on the hill of Cimiez, away from the bustle of Nice. A relaxed hotel, it is renowned for its magnificent views of the city and sea.

Château de la Chèvre d'Or, Èze

MAP H4 ▪ Rue du Barri ▪ 04 92 10 66 66 ▪ Closed Dec–Feb ▪ www.chevre dor.com ▪ €€€
The Chèvre d'Or perches high above the sea, looking out over clifftop battlements in this beautifully preserved castle-village. Rooms have a panoramic view and each one is decorated with antiques. It has three restaurants (see p110) and a pool and a spa in a pretty setting.

Château du Domaine St-Martin, Vence

MAP G4 ▪ Av des Templiers ▪ 04 93 58 02 02 ▪ www.chateau-st-martin.com ▪ DA ▪ €€€
This palatial hotel is set in manicured grounds on a hilltop site with views of the medieval village and the countryside. It is one of the most impressive places to stay in Provence. It offers superb service and excellent food.

Château de la Messardière, St-Tropez

MAP F5 ▪ Rte de Tahiti ▪ 04 94 56 76 00 ▪ www. messardiere.com ▪ DA ▪ €€€
Set on the outskirts of St-Tropez itself, this seaside palace has a private beach, a luxury spa and a swimming pool. It is undoubtedly among the nicest places to stay on this fashionable part of the coast.

Health and Beauty Spas

Hôtel Jules César, Arles

MAP B4 ▪ 9 bd des Lices ▪ 04 90 52 52 52 ▪ www. hotel-julescesar.fr ▪ DA ▪ €
In 2014, Christian Lacroix set about transforming this 17th-century former Carmelite convent in Arles city centre into a chic, boutique hotel. It has a Cinq Mondes spa and a heated pool in the garden cloister.

Le Mas de la Cremaillère, Gréoux-les-Bains

MAP D3 ▪ Rte de Riez ▪ 04 92 70 40 04 ▪ Closed mid-Dec–Mar ▪ www.mas cremailleregreoux.com ▪ €
A range of spa packages at the sulphur-rich thermal springs of Gréoux-les-Bains is available to guests in this farmhouse-hotel with a swimming pool, golf practice range and a restaurant noted for its Provençal menu.

Hôtel le Couvent des Minimes, Mane

MAP D3 ▪ Chemin des Jeux de Maï ▪ 04 92 74 77 77 ▪ www.couventdes minimes-hotelspa.com ▪ €€
This beautiful former convent boasts the first L'Occitane hotel spa, along with a pool, an aromatic garden and a selection of restaurants and bars.

Le Mas de Pierre, St-Paul-de-Vence

MAP G4 ▪ 2320 rte des Serres ▪ 04 93 59 00 10 ▪ www.lemasde pierre.com ▪ DA ▪ €€
Located in the beautiful countryside outside of St-Paul-de-Vence, this luxurious four-star hotel has been designed to help its guests relax. Facilities include a rose garden with stunning views, a hammam and a pool.

Le Mas de la Rose, Orgon

MAP C3 ▪ Rte d'Eygalières ▪ 04 90 73 08 91 ▪ www. mas-rose.com ▪ €€
Set in a vast park of pines, lavender and olive groves, these 17th-century stone *bergeries* (farm buildings) have been transformed into the chic rooms of an elegant hotel.

Les Rosées, Mougins

MAP G4 ▪ 238 Chemin de Font Neuve ▪ 04 92 92 29 64 ▪ www.les rosees.com ▪ €€
A haven of peace and beauty: you can choose between four differently decorated suites in a medieval farmhouse, or a romantic, shabby-chic gypsy caravan at the bottom of the garden.

Hôtel Sezz

MAP F5 ▪ 151 rte des Salins, St-Tropez ▪ 04 94 55 31 55 ▪ www.saint-tropez.hotelsezz.com ▪ DA ▪ €€€
Rooms at this chic and minimalist hotel, just outside St-Tropez, all come with private garden terraces and outdoor showers. There's a spa and an idyllic palm-lined pool, plus a free shuttle service into town.

La Maison de la Sorgue, Île-sur-la-Sorgue
MAP C3 ▪ 6 rue Rose Goudarde ▪ 06 87 32 58 68 ▪ www.lamaison surlasorgue.com ▪ €€€
Furnishings from around the world and cutting-edge mod cons fill rooms and suites in this stunning 17th-century town house, with a secret garden and pool by the river.

Tiara Yaktsa Côte d'Azur
MAP G4 ▪ 6 bd de l'Esquillon, Théoule-sur-Mer ▪ 04 92 28 60 30 ▪ www.yaktsa.tiara-hotels.com ▪ DA ▪ €€€
Perched amid verdant tropical gardens on the wild Esterel coast, this relaxing hideaway oozes Oriental chic. It has bars, restaurants, a private beach and spa access.

Super Hideaways

Hôtel les Deux Rocs, Seillans
MAP F4 ▪ Pl Font d'Amont ▪ 04 94 76 87 32 ▪ www.hoteldeuxrocs.com ▪ No air conditioning ▪ €
Located in a perfectly preserved medieval hill village, this is charming in an old-fashioned way. It has a delightful terrace on a tiny cobbled square, and a restaurant serving great Provençal cooking.

Hôtel Villa la Roseraie, Vence
MAP G4 ▪ 128 av Henri Giraud, rte de Course-goules ▪ 04 93 58 02 20 ▪ www.villaroseraie.com ▪ €
This friendly small hotel has a pool and gardens, and the rooms are charming. It's ideal for a romantic weekend away at an affordable price.

Moulin de la Camandoule, Fayence
MAP F4 ▪ Chemin de Notre-Dame-des-Cyprès ▪ 04 94 76 00 84 ▪ www.camandoule.com ▪ No air conditioning ▪ DA ▪ €
A swimming pool shaded beneath trees, excellent food and a delightful location hidden away among vines and pines make this converted olive mill one of the most peaceful and pleasant places to stay.

Le Cagnard, Cagnes-sur-Mer
MAP G4 ▪ Rue Sous-Barri ▪ 04 93 20 73 22 ▪ www.lecagnard.com ▪ €€
Only a few minutes' drive from the hurly-burly of the Riviera, Le Cagnard is a luxury inn, with lovely rooms in a medieval building, sweeping views and a fine restaurant. All this, and it's located in a pretty village smothered in purple bougainvillea.

Grande Bastide, St-Paul-de-Vence
MAP G4 ▪ Rte de la Colle ▪ 04 93 32 50 30 ▪ www.la-grande-bastide.com ▪ No air conditioning ▪ €€
This converted country house is just outside St-Paul-de-Vence (though it's too far to walk, except for the most energetic). It is calm, friendly and peaceful, with a pool under palm trees and an immaculately kept garden. The rooms and suites are furnished and decorated in Provençal-style fabrics, and there are beautiful views.

La Pérouse, Nice
MAP P5 ▪ 11 quai Rauba Capeu ▪ 04 93 62 34 63 ▪ www.leshotelsduroy.com ▪ €€
This hidden luxury retreat has one of the best views of Nice's lovely promenade. Choose a sea-view room with its own terrace. There's a pretty dining courtyard and a rooftop hot tub as well.

La Riboto de Taven, Les-Baux-de-Provence
MAP B4 ▪ Le Val d'Enfer ▪ 04 90 54 34 23 ▪ www.riboto-de-taven.fr ▪ DA ▪ €€
The "valley of hell" may seem an unlikely location for a romantic hideaway, but the Riboto de Taven, beneath the twisted rocks of the Val d'Enfer, is just that. A troglodyte apartment, magnificent scenery, gardens and a pool add to its appeal.

La Villa Mauresque, St Raphaël
MAP F5 ▪ 1792 rte de la Corniche, Boulouris ▪ 04 94 83 02 42 ▪ www.villa-mauresque.com ▪ €€
On a secret cove near St-Raphaël, this Moorish-style villa was built for a pasha in 1860. In 2013 it was restored as a superb luxury hotel, immersed in lush, exotic gardens.

La Ponche, St-Tropez
MAP F5 ▪ 3 rue des Remparts ▪ 04 94 97 02 53 ▪ Closed Nov–mid-Mar ▪ www.laponche.com ▪ €€€
Stylish, individual and hidden in a tiny square with a view of the fishing port, it is the perfect place to escape the bustle of the town in summer.

Value-for-Money Hotels

Le Benvengudo, Les-Baux-de-Provence
MAP B4 ■ Vallon de l'Arcoule ■ 04 90 54 32 54 ■ www.benvengudo.com ■ €

This charming hotel proves that value is not all about price: it has comfortable, beautifully decorated rooms (some with their own large terrace), a pool, garden, restaurant and tennis court, and all in lovely surroundings.

Hôtel Les Allées, Cannes
MAP G4 ■ 6 rue Emile-Négrin ■ 04 93 39 53 90 ■ www.hotel-des-allees.com ■ €

Could this small hotel, tucked away in a narrow street not far from the yacht harbour, be the best bargain in Cannes? Rooms are simple but clean and bright (some have balconies with a sea view), with phone, TV and Internet connection, and service is friendly.

Hôtel Ambassador, Monaco
MAP H4 ■ 10 av Prince-Pierre ■ 00 377 97 97 96 96 ■ www.ambassadormonaco.com ■ €

This budget hotel could not be better located, right in the very heart of Monaco, at the foot of the Prince's Palace. All the rooms are well equipped, with a TV, hairdryer and Internet access, and the on-site restaurant serves basic Italian cuisine, including good, inexpensive pizzas.

Hôtel le Calendal, Arles
MAP B4 ■ 5 rue Porte de Laure ■ 04 90 96 11 89 ■ www.lecalendal.com ■ DA ■ €

A colourful place to stay in a colourful city, the Calendal is brightly decorated and has a pretty, shady garden café and a comfortable tearoom. Some of the more expensive rooms have terraces and all are air conditioned, making this three-star hotel a great-value place to stay in expensive Arles.

Hôtel La Jabotte, Cap d'Antibes
MAP G4 ■ 13 av Max-Maurey ■ 04 93 61 45 89 ■ www.jabotte.com ■ No air conditioning ■ €

With its clean, bright rooms and chalets and good location, La Jabotte is one of the better bargains in upmarket Antibes. It also has its own car park – quite a rarity in Cap d'Antibes.

Hôtel le Richelieu, Marseille
MAP C5 ■ 52 Corniche Kennedy ■ 04 91 35 78 78 ■ www.hotel-marseille-richelieu.com ■ No air conditioning ■ €

This affordable hotel on the Marseille waterfront has some rooms with balconies and lovely sea views, plus a nice breakfast terrace, a ground-floor terraced restaurant, and a pay-to-use beach just across the road.

Le Windsor, Nice
MAP H4 ■ 11 rue Dalpozzo ■ 04 93 88 59 35 ■ www.hotelwindsor-nice.com ■ €

Exotic Oriental decoration, rooms with frescoed ceilings, a swimming pool surrounded by palm trees and an English-style pub, come at an affordable price in this unassuming-looking hotel.

Hôtel Splendid, Cannes
MAP G4 ■ 4 rue Félix Faure ■ 04 97 06 22 22 ■ www.splendid-hotel-cannes.fr ■ €€

Value for money doesn't always mean cheap, but the Splendid, centrally located close to the yacht harbour, is an impressive hotel and is a bargain by Cannes standards.

Gîtes and Chambres d'Hôtes

La Bastide Rose, Salernes
MAP E4 ■ Quartier du Gaudran ■ 04 94 70 63 30 ■ www.bastide-rose.com ■ No credit cards ■ €

This striking pink-painted farmhouse among vineyards and orchards offers three apartments, two gîtes, two chambres d'hôtes and a pool. Each room has its own kitchenette and terrace.

Le Gîte de Chasteuil, Castellane
MAP F3 ■ Hameau de Chasteuil ■ 04 92 83 72 45 ■ www.gitedechasteuil.com ■ No credit cards ■ No air conditioning ■ €

This delightful bed-and-breakfast is high on a hillside in a tiny hamlet close to the east end of the Canyon du Verdon, with mountain views. For walkers, the GR4 long-distance footpath passes right through the village. Each bedroom has its own bathroom, and one has a kitchenette.

Le Hameau de Pichovet, Vachères

MAP D3 ▪ Campagne Pichovet ▪ 04 92 73 33 48 ▪ www.hameau-de-pichovet.com ▪ No air conditioning ▪ €
Situated close to the lavender fields of the Luberon National Park, this stone house offers four guest rooms and two apartments. The pool is heated from mid-May to mid-October, and the restaurant provides authentic dishes at a family-style dining table or on the terrace.

Maison du Frêne, Vence

MAP G4 ▪ 1 place du Frêne ▪ 04 93 24 37 83 ▪ www.lamaisondufrene. com ▪ €
A delightful melange of Baroque, Pop Art and kitsch fills this arty 18th-century town house in the centre of Vence, opposite, appropriately enough, the Museum of Modern Art. There are four spacious suites and a shared lounge, and rates include free Wi-Fi and a generous French breakfast.

Le Mas de la Beaume, Gordes

MAP C3 ▪ 04 90 72 02 96 ▪ www.labeaume.com ▪ No air conditioning ▪ €€
Throw open the windows and look out onto the Alpilles mountains or the château of Gordes from this delightful old farmhouse. The three rooms and two suites are individually decorated and furnished with quirky antiques and fine linens. The swimming pool is hidden in an olive grove, and breakfast comes with home-made jams.

La Prévôté, Isle-sur-la-Sorgue

MAP C3 ▪ 4 rue Jean-Jacques Rousseau ▪ 04 90 38 57 29 ▪ www. la-prevote.fr ▪ No air conditioning ▪ €€
"A well-kept secret among friends" is the motto of this B&B, set in a former monastery. Rooms are spacious and stylish, and the gourmet restaurant uses only fresh, local produce.

Les Roullets, Oppède

MAP C3 ▪ 305a chemin de Fontdrèche ▪ 04 90 71 21 88 ▪ www.lesroullets.com ▪ No credit cards ▪ €€
High on the hill of a Roman oppidum, this luxurious six-room B&B occupies a stone-built farmhouse. It has a heated pool and beautiful grounds with a 700-year-old tree.

Camping

Camping Abri de Camargue, Le-Grau-du-Roi

MAP A4 ▪ 320 rte du Phare de l'Espiguette ▪ 04 66 51 54 83 ▪ Closed Oct–Mar ▪ www. abridecamargue.fr ▪ €
This clean, medium-sized camp site is near a sandy beach. It has an indoor and outdoor pool, a play area, cinema, bar, shop and restaurant, and *boules* and tennis courts nearby.

Camping Antipolis, Antibes

MAP G4 ▪ Av du Pylone, La Brague ▪ 04 93 33 93 99 ▪ Closed Oct–Feb ▪ www.camping-antipolis.com ▪ DA ▪ €
The best thing about this enormous, four-star full-service camp site is its location: just outside Antibes, a short walk from the sea and with a local railway station with frequent services into Cannes.

Camping du Domaine, Bormes-les-Mimosas

MAP E5 ▪ 2581 rte de Bénat ▪ 04 94 71 03 12 ▪ Closed Nov–Mar ▪ www.campdu domaine.com ▪ DA ▪ €
A stone's throw from the sea, this leafy five-star family-oriented camp site also rents out bungalows and mobile homes. It has many sports facilities and a free children's mini-club.

Camping le Pesquier, Castellane

MAP F3 ▪ RN 85, rte de Digne-les-Bains ▪ 04 92 83 66 81 ▪ Closed Oct–Mar ▪ www.camping-le-pesquier.com ▪ DA ▪ €
This two-star site has a small pool, and tents are pitched under shady trees.

Camping la Pinède, Grimaud

MAP F5 ▪ RD 14 ▪ 04 94 56 04 36 ▪ www.lapinede-camping.com ▪ Closed Nov–Mar ▪ DA ▪ €
A cheap and cheerful alternative to St-Tropez's hotels – with facilities that include a mini-golf course, a children's play area, a restaurant and a snack bar.

La Merio, St-Martin-Vesubie

MAP G2 ▪ 1344 rte de la Colmiane ▪ 04 93 03 30 38 ▪ Closed Oct–May ▪ www.campinglamerio. sitew.com ▪ No credit cards ▪ €
This small, basic site with space for 40 tents is in the heart of the Parc National du Mercantour.

Index

Acknowledgments

Authors

Robin Gauldie is a travel journalist who has visited Provence regularly since 1972. After several years working for the *Travel Trade Gazette*, Robin is now a freelance journalist and author of more than a dozen guidebooks to destinations ranging from Greece to Goa.

Lancashire-born Anthony Peregrine lives in the Languedoc region of southern France, and works as an author and journalist specializing in food, wine and travel. His work has appeared in the *Daily Telegraph*, *Daily Mail* and BBC Radio 4.

Additional contributors
Dana Facaros and Tristan Rutherford

Publishing Director Georgina Dee
Publisher Vivien Antwi
Design Director Phil Ormerod
Editorial Michelle Crane, Rachel Fox, Fay Franklin, Sally Schafer, Beverly Smart, Hollie Teague, Rachel Thompson, Sophie Wright
Design Richard Czapnik, Bharti Karakoti
Commissioned Photography Demetrio Carrasco, Rough Guides/Michelle Grant, Alan Williams
Picture Research Susie Peachey, Ellen Root, Lucy Sienkowska, Oran Tarjan
Cartography James Macdonald
DTP Jason Little, George Nimmo
Production Nancy-Jane Maun
Factchecker Lyn Parry
Proofreader Susanne Hillen
Indexer Helen Peters
Illustrator Chris Orr & Associates

First edition created by Sargasso Media Ltd, London

Režný 4clb; Santiago Rodríguez Fontoba 16br; Guy Rouget 10cl, 89cl, 90b; Alexander Sandvoss 71tl; Juergen Schonnop 15crb; Richard Semik 29crb, 80ca; Stevanzz 43b; Tramontana 50t; Travelpeter 4cl; Willyvend 61tr; Maren Winter 81tl; Oleg Znamenskiy 49tl; Zorro12 76tl.

La Ferme aux Crocodiles: 63br.

Getty Images: DeAgostini/S. Vannini 2tr, 34-5; Hans Georg Eiben 11crb, 18-9; Peter Zelei Images 2tl, 8-9; M G Therin Weise 25crb.

Hostellerie Bérard: 93cra.

Hotel du-Cap-Eden-Roc: 59br.

Hôtel Restaurant Les Deux Frères: 111cr.

L'Arbre à Bulles: 92cr.

L'Esprit de la Violette: Martial Thiebaut 85cl.

Le Louis XV - Alain Ducasse à l'Hôtel de Paris: Pierre Monetta 66t.

Mary Evans Picture Library: BeBa/Iberfoto 36br.

Monte-Carlo S.B.M. Hotels and Casinos: 11br, 32crb, 32-3, 109cl; Philip Ducap 33cr; JJL Heritier 103tl.

Nice Tourism: J. Kelagopian 71cl.

Palais des Festivals et des Congrès de Cannes: Semec-Fabre 108clb; Semec-Perreard 106b.

Rex by Shutterstock: Chris Hellier 57tr; PhotoAlto 38tl; SIPA 37br, /Isa Harsin 96tl; Universal History Archive/Universal Images Group 41bl; WestEnd6 75t.

Robert Harding Picture Library: Christophe Boisvieux 105bl; Martin Child 87tl; Werner Dieterich 82cl; Godong 19tc; Amanda Hall 20-1; Peter Schickert 127cl; Valery Trillaud 113br; Ken Welsh 115cl.

Office de Tourisme de Saint-Raphaël: G. Derivière 88br.

Sens et Saveurs: 123clb.

The Art Archive: Archaeological Museum Vaison-la-Romaine /Gianni Dagli Orti 28bc.

Toinou: 79tr.

Var Tourisme: JH Walzl 88tl.

Vaucluse Tourisme: 126cl, 129cr, 130cla, Alain Hocquel 28cl.

Photo Villa Arson: Architecte Michel Marot & Ass (1970) 68tl.

Cover

Front and spine: **AWL Images:** Stefano Politi Markovina.

Back: **Dreamstime.com:** 300dpi.ru.

Pull Out Map Cover

AWL Images: Stefano Politi Markovina.

All other images © Dorling Kindersley
For further information see: www.dkimages.com

*As a guide to abbreviations in visitor information blocks: **Adm** = admission charge; **DA** = disabled access; **D** = dinner; **L** = lunch.*

Printed and bound in China

First published in Great Britain in 2002 by Dorling Kindersley Limited 80 Strand, London WC2R 0RL

Copyright 2002, 2017 © Dorling Kindersley Limited

A Penguin Random House Company

16 17 18 19 10 9 8 7 6 5 4 3 2 1

Reprinted with revisions 2003, 2004, 2006, 2008, 2010, 2012, 2014, 2017

ISBN 978 0 2412 6419 5

MIX
Paper from responsible sources
FSC™ C018179
www.fsc.org

SPECIAL EDITIONS OF DK TRAVEL GUIDES

DK Travel Guides can be purchased in bulk quantities at discounted prices for use in promotions or as premiums. We are also able to offer special editions and personalized jackets, corporate imprints, and excerpts from all of our books, tailored specifically to meet your own needs.

To find out more, please contact:

in the US
specialsales@dk.com

in the UK
travelguides@uk.dk.com

in Canada
specialmarkets@dk.com

in Australia
penguincorporatesales@ penguinrandomhouse.com.au

Phrase Book

In an Emergency

Help!	Au secours!	oh sekoor
Stop!	Arrêtez!	aret-ay
Call…	Appelez…	apuh-lay
…a doctor!	…un médecin!	uñ medsañ
…an ambulance!	…une ambulance!	oon oñboo-loñs
…the police!	…la police!	lah poh-lees
…the fire brigade!	…les pompiers!	leh poñ-peeyay

Communication Essentials

Yes/No	Oui/Non	wee/noñ
Please	S'il vous plaît	seel voo play
Thank you	Merci	mer-see
Excuse me	Excusez-moi	exkoo-zay mwah
Hello	Bonjour	boñzhoor
Goodbye	Au revoir	oh ruh-vwar
Good night	Bonsoir	boñ-swar
What?	Quel, quelle?	kel, kel
When?	Quand?	koñ
Why?	Pourquoi?	poor-kwah
Where?	Où?	oo

Useful Phrases

How are you?	Comment allez-vous?	kom-moñ talay voo
Very well,	Très bien,	treh byañ
Pleased to meet you.	Enchanté de faire votre connaissance.	oñshoñ-tay duh fehr votr kon-ay-sans
Where is/are…?	Où est/sont…?	oo ay/soñ
Which way to..?	Quelle est la direction pour..?	kel ay lah deer-ek-syoñ poor
Do you speak English?	Parlez-vous anglais?	par-lay voo oñg lay
I don't understand.	Je ne comprends pas.	zhuh nuh kom-proñ pah
I'm sorry.	Excusez-moi.	exkoo-zay mwah

Useful Words

big	grand	groñ
small	petit	puh-tee
hot	chaud	show
cold	froid	frwah
good	bon	boñ
bad	mauvais	moh-veh
open	ouvert	oo-ver
closed	fermé	fer-meh
left	gauche	gohsh
right	droit	drwah
entrance	l'entrée	l'on-tray
exit	la sortie	sor-tee
toilet	les toilettes	twah-let

Shopping

How much is it?	Ça fait combien?	sa fay kom-byañ
What time…	A quelle heure…?	ah kel urr
…do you open?	…êtes-vous ouvert?	et-voo oo-ver
…do you close?	…êtes-vous fermé?	et-voo fer-may
Do you have?	Est-ce que vous avez?	es-kuh voo zavay

I would like …	Je voudrais…	zhuh voo-dray
Do you take credit cards?	Est-ce que vous acceptez les cartes de crédit?	es-kuh voo zaksept-ay leh kart duh krehdee
This one.	Celui-ci.	suhl-wee-see
That one.	Celui-là.	suhl-wee-lah
expensive	cher	shehr
cheap	pas cher, bon marché,	pah shehr, boñ mar-shay
size, clothes	la taille	tye
size, shoes	la pointure	pwañ-tur

Types of Shop

antique shop	le magasin d'antiquités	maga-zañ d'oñteekee-tay
bakery	la boulangerie	booloñ-zhuree
bank	la banque	boñk
bookshop	la librairie	lee-brehree
cake shop	la pâtisserie	patee-sree
cheese shop	la fromagerie	fromazh-ree
chemist	la pharmacie	farmah-see
department store	le grand magasin	groñ maga-zañ
delicatessen	la charcuterie	sharkoot-ree
gift shop	le magasin de cadeaux	maga-zañ duh kadoh
greengrocer	le marchand de légumes	mar-shoñ duh lay-goom
grocery	l'alimentation	alee-moñtasyoñ
market	le marché	marsh-ay
newsagent	le magasin de journaux	maga-zañ duh zhoor-no
post office	la poste, le bureau de poste, le PTT	pohst, booroh duh pohst, peh-teh-teh
supermarket	le supermarché	soo pehr-marshay
tobacconist	le tabac	tabah
travel agent	l'agence de voyages	l'azhoñs duh vwayazh

Sightseeing

art gallery	la galerie d'art	galer-ree dart
bus station	la gare routière	gahr roo-tee-yehr
cathedral	la cathédrale	katay-dral
church	l'église	l'aygleez
garden	le jardin	zhar-dañ
library	la bibliothèque	beebleeo-tek
museum	le musée	moo-zay
railway station	la gare (SNCF)	gahr (es-en-say-ef)
tourist office	l'office du tourisme	ohfees doo tooreesrn
town hall	l'hôtel de ville	l'ohtel duh veel

Staying in a Hotel

Do you have a vacant room?	Est-ce que vous avez une chambre?	es-kuh voo-zavay oon shambr
I have a reservation.	J'ai fait une réservation.	zhay fay oon rayzehrva-syoñ
single room	la chambre à une personne	shambr ah oon pehr-son
twin room	la chambre à deux lits	shambr ah duh lee
room with a bath, shower	la chambre avec salle de bains, une douche	shambr avek sal duh bañ, oon doosh

double room, with a double bed	la chambre à deux personnes avec un grand lit	shambr ah duh pehr-son avek un gronñ lee

Eating Out

Have you got a table?	Avez-vous une table libre?	avay-voo oon tahbl duh leebr
I want to reserve a table.	Je voudrais réserver une table.	zhuh voo-dray rayzehr-vay oon tahbl
The bill, please.	L'addition, s'il vous plaît.	l'adee-syoñ seel voo play
Waitress/ waiter	Madame, Mademoiselle/ Monsieur	mah-dam, mah-demwahzel/ muh-syuh
menu	le menu, la carte	men-oo, kart
fixed-price menu	le menu à prix fixe	men-oo ah pree feeks
cover charge	le couvert	koo-vehr
wine list	la carte des vins	kart-deh vañ
glass	le verre	vehr
bottle	la bouteille	boo-tay
knife	le couteau	koo-toh
fork	la fourchette	for-shet
spoon	la cuillère	kwee-yehr
breakfast	le petit déjeuner	puh-tee deh-zhuh-nay
lunch	le déjeuner	deh-zhuh-nay
dinner	le dîner	dee-nay
main course	le plat principal	plah prañsee-pal
starter, first course	l'entrée, le hors d'oeuvre	l'oñ-tray, or-duhvr
dish of the day	le plat du jour	plah doo zhoor
wine bar	le bar à vin	bar ah vañ
café	le café	ka-fay

Menu Decoder

baked	cuit au four	kweet oh foor
beef	le boeuf	buhf
beer	la bière	bee-yehr
boiled	bouilli	boo-yee
bread	le pain	pan
butter	le beurre	burr
cake	le gâteau	gah-toh
cheese	le fromage	from-azh
chicken	le poulet	poo-lay
chips	les frites	freet
chocolate	le chocolat	shoko-lah
coffee	le café	kah-fay
dessert	le dessert	deh-ser
duck	le canard	kanar
egg	l'oeuf	l'uf
fish	le poisson	pwah-ssoñ
fresh fruit	le fruit frais	frwee freh
garlic	l'ail	l'eye
grilled	grillé	gree-yay
ham	le jambon	zhoñ-boñ
ice, ice cream	la glace	glas
lamb	l'agneau	l'anyoh
lemon	le citron	see-troñ
fresh lemon juice	le citron pressé	see-troñ presseh
meat	la viande	vee-yand
milk	le lait	leh
mineral water	l'eau minérale	l'oh meeney-ral
oil	l'huile	l'weel

onions	les oignons	leh zonyoñ
orange juice	l'orange pressée	l'oroñzh presseh
pepper	le poivre	pwavr
pork	le porc	por
potatoes	les pommes de terre	pom duh tehr
rice	le riz	ree
roast	rôti	row-tee
salt	le sel	sel
sausage	la saucisse	sohsees
seafood	les fruits de mer	frwee duh mer
snails	les escargots	leh zes-kar-goh
soup	la soupe, le potage	soop, poh-tazh
steak	le bifteck, le steak	beef-tek, stek
sugar	le sucre	sookr
tea	le thé	tay
vegetables	les légumes	lay-goom
vinegar	le vinaigre	veenaygr
water	l'eau	l'oh
red wine	le vin rouge	vañ roozh
white wine	le vin blanc	vañ bloñ

Numbers

0	zéro	zeh-roh
1	un, une	uñ, oon
2	deux	duh
3	trois	trwah
4	quatre	katr
5	cinq	sañk
6	six	sees
7	sept	set
8	huit	weet
9	neuf	nerf
10	dix	dees
11	onze	oñz
12	douze	dooz
13	treize	trehz
14	quatorze	katorz
15	quinze	kañz
16	seize	sehz
17	dix-sept	dees-set
18	dix-huit	dees-weet
19	dix-neuf	dees-nerf
20	vingt	vañ
30	trente	tront
40	quarante	karoñt
50	cinquante	sañkoñt
60	soixante	swasoñt
70	soixante-dix	swasoñt-dees
80	quatre-vingts	katr-vañ
90	quatre-vingt-dix	katr-vañ-dees
100	cent	soñ
1,000	mille	meel

Time

one minute	une minute	oon mee-noot
one hour	une heure	oon urr
half an hour	une demi-heure	urr duh-me urr
one day	un jour	urr zhorr
Monday	lundi	luñ-dee
Tuesday	mardi	mar-dee
Wednesday	mercredi	mehrkruh-dee
Thursday	jeudi	zhuh-dee
Friday	vendredi	voñdruh-dee
Saturday	samedi	sam-dee
Sunday	dimanche	dee-moñsh